D0573900

The Maui Millionaires

Discover the Secrets Behind the World's Most Exclusive Wealth Retreat and Become Financially Free

DAVID FINKEL
DIANE KENNEDY, CPA

John Wiley & Sons, Inc.

Published by John Wiley & Sons, Inc., Hoboken, New Jersey.
Published simultaneously in Canada.

For general information on our other products and services or for technical support, please contact our Customer Care Department within the United States at (800) 762-2974, outside the United States at (317) 572-3993 or fax (317) 572-4002.

Wiley also publishes its books in a variety of electronic formats. Some content that appears in print may not be available in electronic books. For more information about Wiley products, visit our web site at www.wiley.com.

The following trademarks are the exclusive property of Maui Millionaires, LLC and are used with permission: Maui Millionaires™, Maui Millionaire™, Maui Millionaire Big Dream Game™, The Five Wealth Factors™, Maui Wealth Scorecard™, Wealth Map™, Maui Wealth Leverage Strategies™, Maui Wealth Leverage Strategy™, Maui Financial Freedom Formula™, Maui Millionaires Wealth Mentorship Program™, Maui Hats™, The Polarity Transformer™, Maui Financial Freedom Score™, Wealth Accelerators™, Level Three Wealth Model™, The Earned Income Trap™.

The following trademarks are the exclusive property of Maui Mastermind (NV), LLC and are used with permission: Maui Mastermind™, The World's Most Exclusive Wealth Retreat™, The Most Exclusive Wealth Retreat In the World™.

The following trademarks are the exclusive property of New Edge Financial, LLC and are used with permission: Wealth Operating System™, The R-Score™, The S-Factor™, Wealth Factor Test™.

Library of Congress Cataloging-in-Publication Data:

Finkel, David
    The Maui millionaires : discover the secrets behind the world's most exclusive wealth retreat and become financially free / David Finkel, Diane Kennedy.
       p. cm.
    ISBN-13: 978-0-470-04537-4 (cloth)
    ISBN-10: 0-470-04537-X (cloth)
    1. Wealth—United States.   2. Millionaires—United States.   I. Finkel, David.
  II. Kennedy, Diane.
  HC110.W4K46   2007
  332.024'01—dc22

                                                2006015378

Printed in the United States of America.

10 9 8 7 6 5 4 3 2 1

This book is dedicated to all those Maui Millionaires out there who share their light and wealth with the world. You create incredible value through your businesses and investments and are a blessing to the world. We are honored to be a part of your lives.

CONTENTS

PART ONE
Maui Wealth Leverage Strategy One: Upgrade Your *Wealth Operating System!*

PART TWO
Maui Wealth Leverage Strategy Two: Dream Big!

PART SIX
The Final Inch

How an Ex-Music Teacher Became a Maui Millionaire— And How You Can, Too!

When David and Diane first invited me to be one of the guest Stars at their exclusive Maui Mastermind™ event, I never imagined that it would impact so many lives so deeply.

At that time I had a close friendship with Diane, whom I respected and admired a great deal, but I truly had no idea of the synergy and chemistry that she and David created with their one-of-a-kind wealth retreat.

There it was, in one concentrated five-and-a-half-day period, a presentation of all the core wealth secrets that had taken me decades to figure out on my own, through painful trial and error.

You see, I started off my career as a music teacher at Central Oregon College. As you can imagine, being a music teacher wasn't exactly the highest-paying profession. But I loved teaching music. So I started a small part-time business in the direct sales industry.

I never would have guessed how that one small decision would change my life forever. I started off with no background in business, with little more than a dream and a desire to earn a little extra income and to help people along the way.

Fast-forward many years to today. My business now has foreign affiliate companies in 50 countries on five continents. I get to work with thousands and thousands of associates all over the world, helping them build their successful businesses.

For me, the game has shifted over the years. I started my business because I wanted to earn some extra income. As my business took off my vision shifted. I've learned that the bed can only be so soft. Today I still play full-out in the business world, but with a different end in mind. It's no longer about me, but about the people and causes that I can help through my businesses.

That's why I feel so aligned with David and Diane and the participants in Maui. They take risks, dream big, and give back to the world. Take the example of Bonnie, whom I met at the Maui Mastermind event last year. She donated the money for shoes for 250 orphans in Cape Town, South Africa. In fact, she invited them on the cruise ship *Crystal Serenity* for the day. Not only did this give them a unique experience, but it opened up dreams for them as the captain told them he often hired South African young people and encouraged them to study and do well in school so they could interview in the future. It's always rewarding to not only help kids in the here and now, but to open up a new future in their imaginations.

I like to say that my two traveling companions are grace and gratitude. I am grateful for my involvement with Maui and being named an honorary Maui Millionaire™.

I was thrilled when I learned that David and Diane had finally decided to share the secrets from Maui with a larger audience by writing this book. I, for one, have been waiting both to read it and to get copies for my business associates and friends.

You see, for most people, this book is the closest they'll ever come to the Maui wealth experience. Considering most people simply can't afford the $30,000 price tag of the real Maui Mastermind event, David and Diane have done an amazing job at recreating the Maui magic in the pages of this book.

In fact, they've poured all their wealth-building magic and expertise into this life-changing book so that you can use it as a launching pad to take your wealth building to the next level.

How Common Money Mistakes Keep You Trapped in the Rat Race

If you're working harder and harder just to keep even financially, then it very well could mean that you're making one or more of the common wealth mistakes—mistakes that may be causing you to work harder, feel more stress, struggle just to stay even, and, worst of all, mistakes that cause you to give up on your dreams.

Could be. Because the one element that the world's wealthiest individuals all have in common is how easy it was for them to succeed financially when they finally understood how money *really* works.

The problem is that this is an education that you didn't receive in school. This is training that you never got on the job. In fact, until now there have been only two ways that a lucky few ever received this kind of wealth training. Either they had a wealthy family member or friend share with them the inside secrets to money and wealth, or they stumbled on these powerful secrets themselves through painful trial and error.

But you have in your hands an unprecedented opportunity to tap into the proprietary ideas and strategies of two of the world's brightest wealth masters to help yourself become financially free.

For the past decade David and Diane have been empowering ordinary people to become wealthy, and coaching wealthy people to become super wealthy.

And during that time they have helped literally tens of thousands of people live richer, fuller, wealthier lives. In fact, their collective clients have gone on to earn, enjoy, and share millions and millions of dollars by building businesses and investing.

Now, for the first time ever, David and Diane are letting you in behind the closed doors of their premier wealth event—the Maui Mastermind. Not only will you get to benefit from the secrets of the super wealthy that David and Diane will lay out for you in precise detail, but you'll also be inspired by the personal examples and stories they share from real-life Maui Millionaires™.

The most amazing thing about money and wealth is how easy it is to attract when you've made several key mental shifts.

In this book you'll learn how one Maui Millionaire was able to grow his business by more than 100 percent *per year* since he first came to Maui, increasing its value fivefold!

And you'll also learn how a retired Intel employee built up a rental property portfolio of hundreds of units that are totally managed by outside companies and that pump out thousands of dollars of passive income year after year. And he did it in less than three years!

How is this possible? Because they have learned how to master the hidden game of money. And it's exactly these wealth secrets that have made them and the other Maui Millionaires financially free.

David and Diane share these same secrets in this powerful book so that money and wealth become demystified, simple, and easy for you. You'll be shocked when you learn the key mental shifts that wealthy people use to make building wealth fun and easy.

Can you imagine the peace of mind you'll enjoy knowing that you have your financial situation handled forever?

I know that this is an awful lot to promise, but this book delivers!

Who This Book Is Right For

This book is right for the following three groups of people:

1. Those people who have always dreamed of financial success but never thought it was possible for them before. You'll have a major wealth breakthrough and learn exactly why it's doable for you and the specific action steps you'll need to take to make it happen.

2. Those people who are already working toward financial freedom but who want to accelerate the process so that they achieve it in less time. You'll learn simple strategies to double or triple your effective net worth in 12 months or less!

3. Anyone else who is *intensely* interested in creating financial freedom and abundance for themselves and their families. You'll learn exactly how to do it in a clear, accessible way.

I want to caution you, however. If you're not willing to hear what David and Diane have to teach on creating wealth, especially since it flies in the face of conventional wisdom (which leads the overwhelming majority of the world's population to financial failure), then this book isn't for you. You'll only find the direct, blunt, action-oriented wealth advice extremely frustrating. David and Diane don't pull any punches; they tell you exactly what works, and more importantly, what doesn't.

Also, if it makes you uncomfortable that David and Diane believe that businesses are stronger and more likely to succeed by building generous giving into the fabric of the business, or that they think that the only way to become truly wealthy is to learn to share your wealth as you build it, then this book isn't for you.

Finally, if you're not willing to act on the lessons, strategies, and techniques that David and Diane share with you in this information-rich book, then don't buy it. If hanging around with some of the world's most successful and wealthy individuals has taught me anything, it has taught me this: The starting point for their wealth came at the moment they seized an opportunity and took action. This is your chance to take action and study this book. Then it's going to be up to you to put the powerful ideas and strategies into action to build your own fortune.

I believe that if you're still reading this Foreword, then you are a special person. You're one of those remarkable individuals who takes responsibility for his or her own life and results. And this book was written just for you.

Wherever you are starting from, this book can help you build from there. You were born for more: more wealth . . . more freedom . . . more security.

God bless you and may you prosper along your journey,

Beverly Sallee

ACKNOWLEDGMENTS

The Maui Millionaires is about a new way of living your life fully. To do this requires a lot of people who help enrich it, and that means there are a lot of people to thank.

This book wouldn't have existed without the vision of Laurie Harting and her team at John Wiley & Sons, the determination of Larry Jellen, and the in-the-trenches work of Megan Hughes, Eva Brunnette, and Cape Cod Compositors. We would also like to thank Diana Arsenian, the talented artist at Maui Mastermind who created the iconography you see spaced throughout this book.

We also want to thank the Maui Stars including Elizabeth Kanna, Morgan Smith, Blake Mitchell, Michael Schinner, Stephen and Susan Wilklow, and Beverly Sallee. You are all inspirations and friends.

Next we want to thank *all* of the participants over the past several years at Maui Mastermind. Your commitment to building wealth and doing good in the world has inspired us to write this book and keep sharing these ideas. We savor our connection with you and are humbled by your energy and ambition.

Our deepest gratitude to the team that makes all of this possible: To Scott, our partner, who is simply in a class of his own; none of this would be without you. To Amy, who is the ultimate Blue Hat organizer with a heart bigger than Maui. To Larry, Gabe, and Monica, thank you for the late nights and last-minute solutions you endlessly supply to make Maui so special.

We also want to acknowledge the breakthrough work that Edward De Bono has done with thinking process and group interactions, the theory of which provided the foundation for the six Maui Hats™.

In addition, David would like to acknowledge:

My world-class teammate Judy. You help me manage the chaos of so many different business ventures in a way that feels fun, smooth, and engaging. Thank you for your commitment to our goals and mission. Together we make the ultimate businessperson.

To my personal mastermind team, you know who you are, thank you for sharing your insights, support, and lives with me. I draw great strength from you and cherish our bond.

xvi ACKNOWLEDGMENTS

To my personal mastermind team, you know who you are, thank you for sharing your insights, support, and lives with me. I draw great strength from you and cherish our bond.

A big thank you and hug to my friends: Mark, Trish, Liz, Cyrus, Jonathon, Kirsten, Steve, Stephen, Michael, Nate, Maggie, Karimjeet, Darcy, Eric, Luz, Blake, Kathleen, Stephanie, and my family. You make my life so much richer and I treasure you.

Finally, to Heather. You are the most important person on the planet to me and I love you with all my heart, body, and soul. You truly are my forever.

In addition, Diane would like to acknowledge:

My personal mastermind group distilled the principles that make my life bigger than I thought possible. Thank you to my mastermind partners Scott Richey, Larry Garcia, Curtis Oakes, and Christine Harvey. You bring a vision to building wealth, enjoying it, and sharing it, that pushes me further.

Every day I try to live up to the standard set by a woman I admire very much—Beverly Sallee. Thank you for setting the bar so high.

None of this would be possible if my businesses didn't run so smoothly. Thank you to the great partners I have in Scott Mertens, Amy DeMeritt (formerly Foxy), Monica Martinez, Chad Parsley, Julie Hill, and Patti Draper. My household runs joyfully because of Mimy.

And the purpose to do any of this comes from the richness of life I experience with my family: my husband Richard, our son David, our four dogs, and a skink.

Thank you all.

Meet the Maui Millionaires

Imagine that you received a letter inviting you to apply for one of a handful of seats at *the world's most exclusive wealth retreat™*. The qualification process included two interviews; the final selection interview was with one of the event's founders who would either accept or deny your application right there on the spot. And to even qualify to get an interview slot you had to show that you had the financial resources to pay for the $30,000 per couple price tag.

Would you even dare to apply? Would you be skeptical that any wealth event could really be worth that kind of money? Would you be scared that if they did accept you, you would be out of your depth?

Well, this is exactly the situation that 36 wealth building teams faced for that first year's Maui Mastermind event. Over the years, they and other new Maui participants have come back to Maui again and again to spend five-and-a-half concentrated days focused on building wealth, networking with other like-minded individuals, and creating ways to give back to people and charities around the world.

Since each year over 75 percent of the participants sign up on the spot to come back the next year, the Maui Mastermind events (held twice a year) are usually sold out a year in advance. In fact, the Maui Mastermind community has grown into the world's premier wealth-building community.

They host regular Maui Reunions; they mastermind together on business and investing opportunities; they do charitable projects together; and most importantly, they have grown deep friendships that are one of life's most precious gifts.*

Now, for the first time ever, we are going to pull back the curtains from around this amazing experience and share with you some of the most powerful insights, strategies, and stories of the Maui Mastermind, and welcome you to our community of wealth builders. In fact, you'll learn about all five of the core Maui Wealth Leverage Strategies™.

For most people, this book is the closest they'll ever come to the Maui wealth experience. We've done our best to pour all the wealth-building magic and expertise we have into the pages of this book so that you can use it as a launching pad to take your wealth building to the next level.

Why We Wrote This Book

As you'll learn in the pages of this book, one core belief of Maui Millionaires is that by giving to the world we are able to enjoy and expand our wealth. This is the driving reason we felt compelled to write this book. We didn't feel satisfied or fulfilled any longer keeping such life-changing, proven technology, insights to our small core group of elite clients. We felt that it was time to share this information in an easy, accessible, immediately applicable way with the world . . . hence this book.

We want to inspire and empower you to become a Maui Millionaire. We want to demonstrate how easy it really is to become exceptionally wealthy, and to show you how to healthfully share that wealth with the world. We want to help you not just earn the money, but to do it in a way that empowers you to live the life of your dreams. To have the money *and* the freedom, to have the money *and* great relationships, to have the money *and* to make a difference in the world, to have the money *and* to live a life that matters, to have the money *and* to have a fulfilling spiritual life, and finally, to have the money *and* to enjoy peace of mind.

---

*Would you like to find out how you can connect with this positive and supportive community of peers? Check out the Appendix for complete details or visit **www.MauiMillionaireBook.com**.

As the founders and guardians of the world's premier wealth-building community, we see it as our mission to empower generations of wealth builders to create, maintain, enjoy, and share great wealth.

The Three Levels of Wealth

There are three levels of wealth. First, and most importantly, there is the level of *being*. This is where you *feel* wealthy, abundant, and at peace. When you enjoy this kind of grounded wealth, it's easy for you to move to the second level of wealth: *doing*. When you have wealth at this action level, you are truly doing what you love and what you are most passionate about. When you start with a firm foundation of wealth as a way of being in the world, and translate that into doing and consistent action, the third and final level of wealth is automatic—*achieving*.

That's why this book doesn't focus on the money. Are you ready for a secret? It's not about the money. It never was, and it never will be. Maui Millionaires know that it's about the person you are being. When you are living as your best self, it's easy to consistently take the necessary action steps to create all the wealth you desire. What's more, you do it by doing what you love to do.

All Maui Millionaires do what they love. It's one of the key "ahas" that all Maui Millionaires have—when you are being your best self and doing what you love, wealth flows to you in abundance.

Alas, most wealth seekers have it all backwards. They think that if only they could have the money, then they could finally do what they love to do. Then they would finally feel happy and fulfilled. But that's backwards. It's like sitting in front of an empty fireplace and saying, "If only I had heat, then I would find some wood and light a match to it."

To get heat you must first start with the wood—at the level of being. Then you need to take action. In this case, it means lighting the match and touching it to the kindling (doing). This results in a fire (achieving). But all wealth begins back with the wood—with the person you are being at any given moment.

The tragic part is that most people put off living until some far future date called "retirement," when they will finally have a chance to do the things they love, so that they can be happy.

Would you answer a job ad that read: "Wanted: committed individual to come work for us for 40+ years doing something you don't love, in an environment that is stressful and toxic, so that when you reach age 65 you can finally retire on half your income (or less) and live out the rest of your years in relative grayness"?

Hundreds of millions of workers around the world applied for and got exactly that job. They don't understand that wealth is an art, and like any art it must be practiced and focused on in order to be mastered. Maui Millionaires have all learned to master this art of building, maintaining, enjoying, and sharing great wealth. It's exactly this precious skillset that you will learn to master in the pages of this book.

Sit up, and pay attention as if your financial life depended on what we are about to share with you, because it quite literally does. If you don't get—in your head and in your heart—what we are about to share with you in this book, you will be poor or, at best, middle income, but never wealthy. And you'll never enjoy the freedom, time, and control of your own life, that comes to you when you are a Maui Millionaire.

So just what does it mean to be a Maui Millionaire, and why is being a Maui Millionaire so different from any plain, ordinary millionaire? Let's face it, given the choice between being a millionaire or not, we think you should choose the millionaire option. But we both recognize that being just a millionaire isn't enough to guarantee success and happiness in life. We want to help you become a Maui Millionaire. And speaking from our personal experiences, being a Maui Millionaire is much more fun, fulfilling, and rewarding.

What Is Wealth?

To many, wealth is equated with money. To other people, wealth is a state of spiritual grace. To others, it is never having to ask how much something costs.

We define wealth as having an abundance of money, love, health, fulfillment, and joy. Wealth is definitely about having the money, but it's more than the money. It's a feeling that you have more than enough, an abundance of time, energy, and options. When you are wealthy you have healthy and fulfilling relationships with people that you love. You have an abiding piece of mind that comes from a balance of integrity, faith, laughter, and a sense that you are meaningfully contributing to the world.

Wealth is broken down into six main areas.

1. *Financial Wealth:* your financial net worth, passive cash flow, active cash flow, and financial prospects.

2. *Emotional Wealth:* self-understanding, acceptance, and love; satisfying and healthy relationships with other people; a sense of joy and happiness.

3. *Spiritual Wealth:* a satisfying connection to a deeper meaning or higher power*; a sense of fulfilling your life's purpose; peace of mind.

4. *Physical Wealth:* a feeling of vitality, energy, and physical well-being.

5. *Intellectual Wealth:* a sense of curiosity and eagerness for learning; intellectual growth and positive challenges.

6. *Time Wealth:* a feeling of abundance of time in your life; a healthy balance between all areas of your life.

Maui Millionaires don't just have the money; they also have the quality relationships that enhance it. Maui Millionaires don't just have the money; they also have the best health they are able to create to provide the vitality to fuel their life. Maui Millionaires don't just have the money; they have the peace of mind that comes from living an integral life in pursuit of passions that matter. And finally, Maui Millionaires don't just have the money; they also have the time to enjoy it!

Ordinary millionaires focus on the money. They build businesses and grow their net worth in ways that require a great deal of their focus and life energy to maintain. Also, many ordinary millionaires don't get the deep enjoyment and satisfaction that they could easily have along with their money. Finally, most ordinary millionaires will never feel free. They feel tied to the wheel of earning more money, or the fear of losing the money they have.

Maui Millionaires on the other hand have what we call *Money Plus*.

---

*Throughout the book you will notice references to faith and God, and what it means to have a real connection to a higher power or deeper meaning in life. We both feel strongly that this is an essential aspect of real wealth, and at the same time we want to be very respectful on this subject because there are different ways to experience the mystery and divine in life. For us, we relate to this experience as God, for others it's a deep connection to nature or love. However you relate to this beauty in your life, we want you to embrace it and know that we respect your views. It's interesting to note that the overwhelming majority of Maui Millionaires have a very deep spiritual life that includes a strong and meaningful faith in God, however they conceptualize or experience God.

Maui Millionaires Have "Money Plus"

They have money *plus* time and freedom to enjoy it.

They have money *plus* the people to share it.

They have money *plus* the health to fuel it.

They have money *plus* the meaning to magnify it.

They have money *plus* the peace of mind to sustain it.

In essence what this book is about is helping you not just make a lot of money (although we have written the book to definitely help you do that), but, more importantly, to build your financial empire in such a way that you have total wealth: physical, mental, emotional, spiritual, temporal, and yes, financial wealth too.

The essence of wealth is three things. First it is a feeling of abundance. It's the knowledge that you have more than you'll ever need. This allows you to let go of the financial fears that paralyze most people, and make better choices for yourself in your life. Second, it is a feeling of gratitude and appreciation. In one real sense, to feel wealthy all you have to do is to take the time to truly appreciate all that you have, and with this awareness comes a deep sense of gratitude that is such an important part of real wealth. And, finally, wealth is the consistent presence of peace of mind. When we live in accord with our deepest values and deal with ourselves and the world with integrity; when we learn to laugh at our own silliness and not take life too seriously; when we feel our connection to a deeper meaning or higher power, then being wealthy is easy and automatic.

Being a Maui Millionaire means that you build your financial wealth in such a way that it promotes your wealth in other areas. This leads to total wealth.

This book is all about the strategies and technologies that you can apply to build your wealth to become a Maui Millionaire. You'll learn how to literally reprogram your wealth beliefs so that financial success is practically guaranteed. You'll also learn the most powerful wealth-creation models and strategies so that you plan and build your wealth on a strong foundation. And finally, you'll learn the practical steps and techniques to build your wealth the right way—fast and balanced, healthy and joyous.

Along the way we'll share with you real-life stories of how we and many of our clients became Maui Millionaires, so that you can learn from real-world references.

The road won't be easy, but the rewards will be worth every ounce of effort you expend along the way. Are you ready to join us on this dynamic adventure to create the life of your dreams as you step up and become a Maui Millionaire? Good, let's get started then!

MAUI WEALTH LEVERAGE STRATEGY ONE:
Upgrade Your
Wealth Operating System!

CHAPTER 1

How Wealthy Are You?

t's so easy in today's fast-paced world to get swept away in the activity of living and never stop to make the time to look at the bigger parts to your life. Let us ask you a direct question: How wealthy are you? On a scale from one to ten, with one being extremely poor and ten being massively wealthy, how wealthy are you?

Jot that number down in the box below.

Now, before we continue, let us ask you a radically different series of questions: What are you most grateful for in your life? Who are the people who matter most to you? What are the experiences you are so thankful to have had?

Some people think that everything has its price. Well, if that's true, how much would it take for you to sell your ability to see? Would you accept a million dollars in return for your ability to see? How about ten million dollars?

What about your ability to move? How much would you sell your ability to walk for? How about your ability to move your arms? Would you trade them for any amount of money?

What about your past? What would you sell all your memories for? Would you trade all your memories, good and bad, leaving you bereft of any past, for a million dollars?

What about the love of your friends and family? What would your price be to trade for these precious relationships?

Just take a moment to reflect on the people, things, abilities, and experiences you are most grateful for in your life.

Now, how wealthy are you *really*? On a scale from one to ten, how wealthy are you when you stop and look at the full picture of your life?

In our experience, the average person's real wealth score goes up by 30 percent just by doing this one short exercise. How is it possible that you can become so much more wealthy so quickly and with such little effort? That is because wealth is really a mental and emotional game that over time manifests in the physical world. And in the inner game of money, small shifts at key leverage points can instantly increase your wealth—without struggle, without effort, and without complicated formulas.

That's what *The Maui Millionaires* is all about—helping you win the inner game of money so that you master the real secrets to wealth and financial success.

This book is guaranteed to surprise many and shock some. Why is that? Because most people are trained to think that money is something you earn by what you do. That is just not so. Wealth is attracted by the person that you are. While it's true you earn the money from focused action, the real driving force for building great wealth is the person you are.

Most people get it all wrong. They say if only they could have the things they want to have it would allow them to do the things they want to do so that they could be the person they want to be. But that is all backward. In fact, to be truly wealthy the pathway to follow is to focus first on the person you are. This will control the actions you take. Finally, this will result in the things you earn.

This is just one of the flaws in most people's thinking about money and wealth that leads over 95 percent of the population to financial failure.

The Power of a Model

Call it a map, a model, or a metaphor. These are the internal constructs we use to make sense of the world. It's the way we see the world and the results we get in the world. For the moment, we'll call these internal representations of the world around us "models."

A model is a tool to help us understand the world. It's a way we organize and structure experience so that we can simplify and understand some part of the world. We use models all the time in our life to help us more effectively interact with the world. For example, few of us really understand the technical descriptions of how e-mail works. But we do understand the big picture of what it is and how to use it to get the results we want in life by thinking about e-mail like ordinary mail, but only instant (or close to it.) The model of how an ordinary letter gets written, addressed, mailed, delivered, and then opened gives us a structure with which to easily use e-mail to communicate. E-mail is so easy to use because functionally each of the steps we take to use e-mail, even the very names we call the different steps, are directly analogous to ordinary mail. For example, we address an e-mail to a recipient. And we check our e-mail inbox just as we have to check our mail box to see if we've got mail.

Models are so powerful because, once they are accepted, they work below the level of conscious awareness to control how we think about something. In essence, once we accept a specific model as true, then this model melts into the background, and from there it influences how we interact with the world.

So to have the best chance of getting what you want in the world, you need an effective model, which will help you get the results you want. Sadly, many well-intentioned models in the past have been so inaccurate that they have caused great harm.

Here are a couple of examples of old-world models that we have moved beyond.

Old Model: Illness is caused by bad spirits or poisons in the blood.

Actions Taken Based on That Poor Model: Bloodletting.

Results: This old model, and the actions people took, literally killed people. One of those people was the first president of the United States, George Washington, who many historians believe died due to excessive blood loss from well-intentioned doctors who followed this flawed model, trying to cure him of an illness through bleeding him.

Old Model: The world is flat.

Actions Taken Based on That Poor Model: Don't sail too far. Don't explore beyond your boundaries.

Results: Intellectual and technological improvements that come from free trade with other groups was limited. Just think how long Europeans had to wait for chocolate, tomatoes, and corn—all products of the New World!

Old Model: Security comes from finding a great job and working hard to become invaluable.

Actions Taken Based on That Poor Model: Spend excessive amounts of time and energy at the job and acquire skills that help you at that job.

Results: Putting all of your future financial hopes in one basket . . . and then risking losing that basket when you are laid off or the company goes broke due to poor management or fraud, or because of radical changes to your industry.

Old Model: Wealth is a zero sum game In order for you to earn more, someone else has to earn less.

Actions Taken Based on That Poor Model: In the past, laws forbidding sharp practices that meant you couldn't make money in commerce; to this day, the suggestion you did something immoral or unethical if you have wealth.

Results: Small lives with unfulfilled purpose and constant financial pressure.

Old Model: Work really hard for 45 years, then retire and do what you love to do.

Actions Taken Based on That Poor Model: Nose to the grindstone and put off being happy.

Results: Not living in the present and enjoying the relationships, health, spiritual and other gifts you have right now.

If you want to make minor, incremental changes and improvements, work on practices, behaviors, or attitude. But if you want to make significant, quantum improvement, work on paradigms.
—STEPHEN COVEY

The models we accept into our life make up our personal map. This book is all about making key changes to our Wealth Map™ so that making money is easy and automatic. We believe that everyone is born to be a Maui Millionaire; it just takes a few key shifts to set yourself on that path. We believe that the very fact that you found this book means you have everything you need to become a Maui Millionaire. All that's needed is for you to tap into your real wealth-making potential so that you can earn all you've ever dreamed of earning.

We've noticed that many of the people who come to Maui, in the beginning, want it to be all about hard data, content, and information. What they come to realize is that the biggest wealth breakthroughs don't come from information, but rather from a shift in perspective, from a new wealth model. It's this focus on context that has made Maui so powerful, and it's why close to 75 percent of the participants choose to come back year after year.

The Paradox of Knowledge

So many of us think that what we lack is information. If only we knew enough, then we wouldn't be so uncertain or afraid, and then we'd be able to take action and succeed. We think that the way out is to learn more. But, alas—the more we learn, the more we learn that we don't know yet. So we go back and learn more. But again this has the unintended consequence of showing us more things that we now know that we don't know. More information is never the way out, it only leads to more things that we become aware that we don't know. But there is a moment when we know enough. When do you think that moment is?

You know enough when you can get yourself to take positive action knowing that you don't know it all, but that you'll figure it out along the way.

Yes, information and knowledge are critical to success and wealth building. But, and this is a very big but, too many people hide behind their need to learn more when what really is the challenge is that they are scared. One of the most important lessons Maui has taught us is the importance of taking positive action in the presence of our fears. The wealthiest people have all grown their capacity to get more and more comfortable with feeling the feelings of fear. They have become better and better at doing those things they know will make the biggest difference, but that may also scare them.

On one level, that's what Maui is all about—stretching people's comfort zone enough so that they never shrink back to their old dimensions.

It's about creating a powerful and supportive environment within which people can dare to dream the big dreams that once upon a time were just too scary.

David's Story

I've lived a lot of my life looking for ways to play it safe or not feel afraid. I've ended relationships because I was scared that other people would leave me. I've held myself back because I was scared of what it might mean about myself if I committed fully and failed. Over the past several years, I've taken a hard look at that part of me and made some quantum changes. One of the most important was the first of what's come to be known as my Maui Commitments. Each year at Maui those people who want to step up and play full-out make a commitment to do the thing that scares them the most, that, if they could get themselves to do it, they know it would make the biggest difference in their life.

Well, the very first year we started doing this, I was having breakfast on a patio overlooking the Pacific Ocean in Maui. It was a glorious day, and I was enjoying my morning feast, reading a local tourist magazine. One of the articles caught my attention. It talked about how you could scuba dive in the shark tank at the local aquarium. A little background is in order here. I love to swim in the ocean, but ever since I saw the movie *Jaws* I've been terrified of sharks. I'd be out there swimming and I'd hear that "da dum . . . da dum . . ." in my head. I'd start to have a mild panic attack. Over the years, I'd learned to talk myself down from that, but it still was a huge fear for me. Well, that morning I decided I should do this shark dive and get over that fear. Notice the language there? *Should*. Well, I conveniently let that idea slip from my head until the morning of the last day of the event. There I was, right before I was to get up on stage and spend the morning teaching people about how to make huge shifts in their lives and personal fortunes, when I knew I couldn't face them unless I walked my own talk. So that very morning, I made my first-ever Maui Commitment. I explained to them my fear of sharks and what it would mean to me if I could face it.

(continued)

David's Story *(continued)*

I poured out my heart about how I was no longer willing in my life to ever again let fear rule me. I committed to them that by next year's Maui I was going to swim with sharks. What a glorious moment it was, with people cheering and inspired to make big commitments in their own lives.

But then I went home . . . and the thought of swimming in a tank full of sharks didn't quite seem so warm and fuzzy anymore. Besides, I didn't even know how to scuba dive! I bet you can understand what I did next. I procrastinated. I distracted myself. All the way until six weeks before Maui rolled around again. I think part of me wanted to forget all about playing full-out and just hide under the covers. Maybe I was hoping they would all forget. But I didn't forget. No matter that I had spent the past year doing my best to forget, I knew it was important for me to face my fear, so that I had the experience of doing the thing I was terrified to do and surviving that fear.

I made a call that day to make reservations for myself and a friend, Steve, a returning Maui Graduate, to do the shark swim. In fact, I made the call from the parking lot of a community pool I was about to enter to do my second day of scuba certification!

The morning of the shark swim arrived, and I was scared. Oh, I put on a brave face when I met Steve and his wife Kim that morning at the aquarium, but I was scared. I had only completed the final of my open water dives needed for my certification the day before. But I wasn't going to back out. Sometimes in life, we need that accountability or that grand gesture that means nothing yet means everything. And so, on that Friday morning in December, Steve and I slipped into that large tank filled with over 25 sharks, including several hammerhead sharks and a 12-foot tiger shark. The first minute was all about remembering to breathe—deep breaths, one after the other. But a funny thing happened a few minutes into the dive. A switch flipped in my head from fear into fascination, from abject terror into amazement and wonder. These creatures were so beautiful and graceful.

(continued)

David's Story *(continued)*

I left the tank that morning after 40 minutes of peaceful wonder. (And yes I had all my limbs intact!) I felt so empowered because I did the thing that I feared most. Not only that, I found it was a tremendous joy. As you progress in your wealth building and learn to play at bigger and bigger levels, you will always find things to stretch and scare you. Embrace these opportunities and do the thing you think you can't. A whole new world awaits you each time you do.*

*Would you like to see the video footage of David swimming with the sharks? Then just go to **www.MauiMillionaireBook.com** where you can watch an exclusive video of the shark dive.

> One of the greatest wealth skills you can ever develop is learning to get comfortable with feeling uncomfortable; learning to not be so afraid of feeling afraid.

Meet the Maui Millionaires

Would you know we were Maui Millionaires if you met us? Only if you understood what to look for. Most people would spot Diane as a millionaire for all the wrong reasons. They'd say she must be a millionaire because of the clothes she sometimes wears, the BMW she drives, or for the expensive jewelry she likes. Few people would see David for the millionaire he is because he tends to dress very casually. But it's important to understand that outward dress is seldom a sign of wealth. Instead, if you paid close attention to the clues, you'd know Diane was a Maui Millionaire because of the way she talks about money and wealth. You'd see that David was a Maui Millionaire because of the flexibility and freedom he enjoys in his lifestyle.

Maui Millionaires are easy to spot when you start watching for how they relate to time, wealth, and personal freedom. They have a perspective on wealth that makes it clear that they know they live in an abundant world where they are totally responsible for everything that happens in their lives. This responsibility energizes them as they build the lives of their dreams.

Take the example of Blake, one of the Maui Millionaires who attended the first Maui Mastermind event. Blake was a successful business owner and real estate investor who had built a nice life for himself. But it wasn't tapping into his passion and creativity. It didn't give him an outlet for helping the world. For Blake, Maui was about tearing down the walls of his "nice" life so that he could make room for his big dreams and ambitions. He knew he could never be satisfied with his comfortable life; he had to contribute and create more. Not only did he leave Maui and immediately lead a group of investors through a successful and highly-lucrative condo conversion project, but he sold a large chunk of his business to three of his business partners for an even larger profit, and then used the time to focus on what mattered most to him. He is one of the founders of *Estrellas Para Ninos*, a charity that he and fellow Maui attendees started, to support and care for several orphanages in Juarez, Mexico. Blake began an expression that has held consistent for most all of the participants—"Life before Maui . . . Life after Maui."*

The Maui Magic works even for the Stars at Maui. Take Morgan Smith, one of the Maui Stars who taught at the last three Maui Mastermind events. Morgan is the president and owner of Morgan Financial, a mortgage brokerage company. When Morgan joined the Maui team two years ago his company had 50 branches doing a gross volume of $750 million of loans each year. By the end of the Maui Mastermind held two years later, Morgan Financial had grown to 150 branches in 25 states doing $1.2 *billion* in gross business volume with a team of over 1,150 people on board. In that time, his company's net worth has increased 500 percent! Maui really stretched him. The ideas in this book can do the same for you.

Maybe you're saying, "Sure, Blake and Morgan can do it. After all, they were already very successful financially as the owners of thriving

---

*How would you like to meet the Maui Millionaires? Then go to **www.Maui MillionaireBook.com** and click on the "Meet the Maui Millionaires" link to listen to over six hours of in-depth audio interviews with the Maui Millionaires featured in this book. They'll share exactly how they got started in their wealth building and the key lessons they learned along the way. Just go to **www.MauiMillionaireBook.com** to instantly access these amazing and candid interviews.

businesses before they came to Maui. But there's no way little old me could do it."

Well, then, what about Kelly? She was an officer with the Los Angeles Police Department when she and her husband Rob came to Maui. Before she came to Maui they were $77,000 in credit card debt but committed to building something more for themselves. Kelly's childhood had ingrained a mindset of financial hardship that she didn't know how to get free from. She and Rob came to Maui scared but with a willingness to trust. That's what we're asking you to do right now. For the few hours it takes you to complete this book, reserve your judgment and trust us a little.

That first year's Maui Mastermind was a huge awakening for Kelly. She went back to the mainland and immediately quit her job and jumped full-time into building her investing business. By the end of her third year at Maui, Kelly had been a part of several big deals, including a dozen single-family houses, a condo conversion project, and she had acquired over 200 rental units with professional management teams in place, and she expects to pick up 200 more this year! In fact, her husband Rob, who was also a police officer, quit soon after Kelly started to succeed with her investing. That gave Rob the opportunity to pursue his passion: He began a hand-crafted furniture business. That is what Maui really means—pursuing your passion on your way to building great wealth. If Blake, Morgan, Kelly, and Rob can become Maui Millionaires, then you most certainly can too. And that's exactly what you'll be learning in the next 21 chapters of this book.

What "Maui" Really Means

To us, Maui is not just a beautiful island in the Pacific. Maui is a magic place of possibility where people go to create the life of their dreams. That's true, even if those dreams weren't clear before they arrived.

Maui represents a place where we live as our best and highest selves, and from this best part of us, tap into the true dreams and passions we have about how to live our lives, what goals to go after, and how we can touch the world around us.

We can't run away and live our lives in Maui. That wouldn't be a healthy way to live. Maui isn't about isolating ourselves from the world, but rather, it's about stepping outside the loud, incessant, daily demands of our lives, and regrouping. It's about figuring out what matters most to you and creating the wealth and freedom to enjoy it.

Being a Maui Millionaire isn't about never being afraid; it's about gathering the inner strength to face our fears and move forward in their presence. It's the commitment that we will find a way to make things work, no matter what.

Maui means dreaming big, and understanding that the biggest dream of all is the one that resonates in your heart, no matter what other people say.

An essential part of Maui is opening yourself up to wealth and abundance, and dealing with the internal challenges that this mindset can raise. After all, the best reason to become rich isn't for the money, it's for the person you will become. Stretch to create real wealth, not to have money to spend (although that is fun and useful), but rather to grow as a person. We become wealthy to the degree to which we grow our capacity to contain that wealth and to share that wealth in healthy ways with the world.

Perhaps the biggest part of Maui is the renewal it represents, and the inspiration, support, and accountability we bring home from the Maui community into our daily lives.

Ultimately, Maui is about living a life that matters. It's about growing into the person you really are, at the core of your being. It's about working with mastermind partners to help each other touch the world. It's about dreaming big. And it's about upgrading your Wealth Operating System so that you are ready to receive all the wealth and abundance you deserve.

Many of you who are reading this book have already achieved so much. You've reached many of your career goals, financial goals, health goals, giving goals, or other personal goals. In fact, it might feel like you've reached the top of the building. If this is you, we're hoping that you use this book as a spark to break out and break free of your comfortable prison. So many people are masters of their environments. They have spent a lifetime learning to shape their small world just so, in order that they should never have to feel the twinge of uncertainty. *The Maui Millionaires* is about helping you blast through that false ceiling to feel the aliveness that comes from real growth and taking intelligent chances again. Remember, a big part of wealth is feeling alive and growing each day.

Others of you who are reading this book look at the lifestyle of a Maui Millionaire with desire and awe. That's fine too. *The Maui Millionaires* will stretch your belief level so that you can accomplish much more than you ever thought possible.

David's Story

I was sitting on the couch when Heather came in from shopping for bathing suits a few days before we were flying to Maui for the annual Maui Mastermind event. She showed me six or seven new bathing suits she had purchased, and my first comment was, and every woman reading this book will recognize it for the ignorant comment that it is, "Why did you need more bathing suits?" I mean, she had a whole bunch of perfectly good old ones to choose from. But that's when I found out that the elastic in women's swimming suits stretches out over time to the point that it loses its elasticity. (This never happens with men's bathing suits, since we have drawstrings in the waist.)

In a way, Diane and I hope you find this book to be a tool to stretch you to the point that you are never able to revert back to your same old life. We want for you to experience the thrill of stepping up to live life as it was meant to be lived—full-out and with no excuses. Maybe if we can stretch you far enough in this book, you will never shrink back to the life you used to settle for. After all, you deserve so much more, are capable of so much more, and can share so much more.

Getting Rid of Your Excuses

It never ceases to amaze us the lengths and creativity that we observe people go to to create and maintain their excuses, we mean *reasons*, for why they can't do what they say is most important to them.

If these people would put the same energy, determination, and imagination into doing or changing the thing they are making excuses for, most times they would easily accomplish the very thing they say they wish they could do.

If you're reading this book, then we know you are a person who takes responsibility for your own life and for your results. Wherever you are starting from, we can help you build from there.

How *The Maui Millionaires* Is Laid Out

Time to get into the nitty-gritty details of how this book is laid out so that you can maximize your time reading it to empower you to build your wealth.

The book is laid out in six sections. Five of these sections are the Five Maui Wealth Leverage Strategies™ that will accelerate your wealth building in simple, powerful ways, the results of which you cannot begin to imagine even in your wildest dreams or fantasies. Here are the sections.

Part One: Maui Wealth Leverage Strategy One—Upgrade Your Wealth Operating System!

Learn a powerful five-step process to literally reprogram your belief system about wealth, money, and financial abundance so that making money is easy and automatic. Never again will you unwittingly engage in self-sabotaging wealth-destroying behaviors. In this section you'll learn the key distinctions that will put you in charge of your own wealth program.

Part Two: Maui Wealth Leverage Strategy Two—Dream Big!

We're told to dream no small dreams because there is no power in them. But many of us are so busy with the day-to-day busy-ness of living, that we've forgotten our dreams. Be bold and create those big dreams in the seven important areas of your life to serve as the guiding star for all that you accomplish. Plus, learn how to tap into others' dreams to build a lasting joint venture to accomplish even more.

Part Three: Maui Wealth Leverage Strategy Three—Mastermind Your Way to Millions!

Best of all, you don't need to do it all alone. Discover how to create a highly-functional mastermind group that will push you to even greater accomplishments. You'll learn the five critical elements of a powerful mastermind to keep it operating at the highest possible level for huge positive results.

Part Four: Maui Wealth Leverage Strategy Four—Build Level Three Wealth and Enjoy a Maui Lifestyle!

It's not enough to just make a lot of money. You need to build your wealth in such a way that it truly creates secure and thriving financial freedom. In this section, you'll learn the secret Maui Financial Freedom Formula™ and a breakthrough new system for measuring your *real* financial progress.

Part Five: Maui Wealth Leverage Strategy Five—Tap into Maui Giving to Create a Legacy that Lives On beyond You!

One of the hallmarks of a Maui Millionaire is the sustained giving that he creates throughout his lifetime. There are many reasons for giving: to feel good, because it's the right thing to do, to open doors for expanded business, and simply so that you can live in total certainty you have an abundance of time, talent, and money in your life.

Then, once you've learned these essential strategies and technologies to leverage from where you are to where you want to be, we have one more important section of the book for you.

Part Six: The Final Inch

You'll learn the two secret ingredients behind the fourth dimension of wealth. These two keys are what convert money into wealth, and transform ordinary millionaires into Maui Millionaires. Plus, you'll learn exactly how to put the ideas and strategies you've learned into action to become a Maui Millionaire. All you'll need to do is follow the step-by-step action plan we've designed to lead you to financial abundance and freedom.

Because we know that you will need support, accountability, and coaching along the way, we have created a special *free* $2,495 bonus for readers like you. It's called the Maui Millionaire Wealth Mentorship Program™, and this 90-day online wealth coaching and training system is our gift to you. You heard us right, you get this powerful, proven wealth-building system for *free!* To find out all the details about how you can instantly tap into this valuable bonus to accelerate your wealth building, just go to the Appendix for complete details, or go to **www.MauiMillionaireBook.com** to register right now.

So turn the page and let's begin with the first of the five Maui Wealth Leverage Strategies—upgrading your *Wealth Operating System.*

CHAPTER 2

Your *Wealth Operating System*

Why is it some people are able to make money so easily, while other people struggle to makes ends meet, never able to make or accumulate much financial wealth? Or if they do make it, they aren't able to keep it? Or maybe they're not able to enjoy and share it in healthy ways? Could there be some fundamental difference that empowers wealthy people to build and maintain their wealth in a way that in the past just wasn't common knowledge for the poor and middle class? Could it be that wealthy people really do think differently from the poor and middle class?

The answer is a resounding yes. Wealthy people literally have a different way of thinking about wealth that makes it easy for them to build, maintain, enjoy, and share greater and greater wealth, while poor and middle-class people have a disempowering belief system about money and wealth that makes it almost impossible for them to succeed financially. That is, unless they first change their way of thinking about money, wealth, and riches.

How we go about making money—and maintaining and growing that wealth when we have it—is the direct result of our internal programming on wealth.

Think about a computer for a moment. You have the hardware. This includes your keyboard, mother board, hard drive, and other physical components to the computer. You also have the software that you run on that computer. This includes programs like a word processor or spreadsheet or even several games if one of your kids has anything to say about it.

But this isn't enough for you to actually use your computer and harness the full power it offers you. To do that, you need one more hidden ingredient that works in the background—it's called the "operating system." This special type of software is the critical link between the hardware and the other software and it's what actually allows the software to work in the environment of your hardware to produce a specific outcome.

In a sense, this is a useful model of how we are programmed for wealth. We have specific attributes like our physical body, native intelligence, our memory, our ability to focus, and our natural talents. This is like the hardware of the computer system. We also have specialized knowledge of specific areas like business, or real estate investing, or accounting, or medicine, or sales, or management. This specialized how-to knowledge is the software we run in our heads. The bridge that connects our attributes and abilities with our specialized knowledge to make money is our Wealth Operating System™. Your Wealth Operating System, or W.O.S. for short, is the sum total of your beliefs about money, wealth, and your ability to earn and enjoy it. Over a lifetime these beliefs become internalized, and they control your ability to earn, maintain, and enjoy money.

After many years of teaching people how to make money by building businesses and investing in real estate, there is one simple fact that we have learned about which we are absolutely certain—the wealth you allow yourself to earn, maintain, and enjoy is a direct reflection of your Wealth Operating System. It is quite literally your money blueprint.

As we've just mentioned, wealthy people actually think differently from poor and middle-income people. The reason why wealthy people see wealth in a totally different way from poor and middle-income people is that they are literally running an upgraded W.O.S.

In essence, your Wealth Operating System is the sum total of your beliefs, feelings, and self-created relationship to money, wealth, and financial success. It is colored by your experiences, hopes, fears, and your emotional associations to money and wealth.

The sum total of your emotional associations and beliefs about money and your relationship to it.

Wealth Operating System

Hardware
• Intelligence
• Memory
• Natural Talents
• Energy & Drive

Software
• Specialized Knowledge
• Learned Skills

MAP

IDENTIFY WHAT YOUR CURRENT "W.O.S." IS.

Where Does Your Wealth Operating System Come From?

So who is the programmer who gave you your W.O.S.? Initially, we all pick up our W.O.S. from five places.

First, there is the main influence of our parents who raised us. Next, there are the friends and family members with whom we spent time, especially when we were young. Of course, we need to include the other people with whom we spent time: teachers, coaches, and other influential adults. Then there is the pervasive cultural influence of the mass media we were, and are, exposed to. And finally, there is the collective societal influence of our culture as a whole. All of these forces combine together to lay the foundation for your W.O.S. Over time, you layer on other experiences from your life that add to your W.O.S. But, on the whole, most of us have our W.O.S. firmly programmed during our early years, well before we turn 18.

Roger's Story

Roger's parents grew up in the Depression era. His mother was very frugal. She'd seen what could happen when the bottom fell out, and never wanted that to happen again. The family didn't go on vacations and instead learned how to make do with very little.

For Roger, that meant that he reached a point where he stopped buying real estate, although he was very successful with it. He felt he had enough to support his family and that there was something wrong about wanting more. He didn't need it—so he shouldn't have it. As he looked deeper into the associations that he had because of the W.O.S. of his parents, he realized that those beliefs about money weren't even his. And they certainly weren't helping him become the person that, deep down, he wanted to be.

He became involved in giving back to others and traveled to do hands-on work at orphanages in Mexico. He recognized that there were others who didn't need a hand-out so much as a hand-up. And that would take money and time. He had a new reason to create more wealth in a healthy way. He needed to become a Maui Millionaire. But, first, he had to change his core beliefs about money.

Roger has gone on to create many-fold more wealth, but it all started with that simple shift in his W.O.S.

Here's the key: While our initial W.O.S. was installed when we were young and before we ever consciously chose the W.O.S. we wanted, as adults we can consciously choose and upgrade our W.O.S. so that we can build, enjoy, and maintain great wealth.

You are *not* stuck with your old, outdated, stone-age, depression-era W.O.S. At any time you can upgrade to a newer, more powerful, more abundant, wealthier version. In fact, that is one of the wealth leverage points we'll be focusing on in this book to help you to become a Maui Millionaire.

Many people's W.O.S. is set for hundreds or at best thousands of dollars. But Maui Millionaires have upgraded their W.O.S. to be set for making hundreds of thousands, millions, or even billions of dollars. Think about someone like Bill Gates. What do you think his W.O.S. is set for? Do you think Bill Gates would ever settle for just being a millionaire? No way. His W.O.S. is so powerfully set, he can't help but make billions, enjoy billions, and share billions. (In case you didn't know, he and his wife Melinda are two of the most generous philanthropists of all time. They have donated over 20 billion dollars to charitable causes. Bill attributes his charitable work to a reminder by his mother on his wedding day. On a card to the newlyweds, she wrote, "With great wealth, comes great responsibilities.")*

Sadly, so many people's W.O.S. is set for below zero, and they wonder why they are freezing! They live life afraid of looking at the truth about their financial situation because they are afraid of what they'll see. But this makes about as much sense as never going to the dentist so you won't have any cavities!

For things to get better, you've got to get better. For your financial life to change, you've got to change. And your W.O.S. is the single greatest leverage point in your wealth building. A small, focused investment of time and energy here will pay back huge dividends of money, time, and freedom over many years to come. This is why over a third of the Maui Mastermind event is focused on helping attendees completely upgrade their W.O.S. With this one change, you will quickly and automatically multiply your wealth.

---

*Would you like to learn about history's most generous and remarkable philanthropists? Then go to **www.MauiMillionaireBook.com** for a FREE online workshop spotlighting the world's most generous givers and showing how *you* can make a difference in the world. This will help you associate money and wealth as a means to contribute massively to the benefit of humanity. See the Appendix for details.

David's Story

Did you know that it is actually easier to make $2 to $3 million a year with a business than it is to make $20 to $30 thousand a year with a business? When I first got started in business, I worked long hours for very little money. Not only would it take much of my personal time, but I had to invest much of my emotional energy in just making the business work. Fast forward 10 years. Now, when I start a business, I immediately team up with people who are great at the things I'm not—using the mastermind principle that you will be learning about later in this book. As a result I'm able to build a million-dollar business with a fraction of the time, effort, or emotional energy. This holds true whether it is for a business I am building or a property I am investing in.

For example, about nine months ago I, along with two partners, bought a 320-unit apartment complex for approximately $8 million. Nate, one of my partners in the deal, oversaw the turn-around of this property. At the time I am sharing this story, we have the property in escrow to sell it to another investor for $9.6 million. All totaled, we'll net about $1.3 million for a deal that has been fairly easy to put together. Why wasn't I able to do deals like this when I first started investing in real estate? Because my W.O.S. wouldn't allow it. It was so foreign to my W.O.S., so out of my comfort zone, that I literally never even saw deals like this before. Did deals like this exist 10 years ago? Of course they did, but I wasn't able to even see them, so other investors, with more expansive W.O.S.s, did those deals and profited millions and millions of dollars.

This is the power of your W.O.S. When you upgrade it, you are able to make ten, a hundred, even a thousand times more money, with the same—or many times less—effort!

Now some of you are probably still saying, "Yeah but. . . ." Yeah but it's harder to make more money, to make more money you have to work harder. As if Bill Gates works 1,000 times more hours to earn billions instead of hundreds of thousands or millions. The truth is that it's harder to make less money than it is to make millions because when you are only making a little money you have your whole focus down at the level of survival. It's nearly impossible to become a Maui Millionaire if you leave your focus at the level of survival. It's critical that you raise your awareness to the limitless wealth that is available to you, and to everyone else, so that you can change your focus and see the opportunities that are all around you. For example, did you know it's easier to borrow $4 million to buy an apartment building than it is to borrow $400,000 to buy a house? And often it's easier to raise $5 million to expand your business than it is to raise $50,000.

But wait, you say, to make more money you have to risk more money. Again, this is one of those misleading beliefs that comprise poor and middle-income people's W.O.S. Maui Millionaires all know that it is possible to invest with lower risk and get a higher return, if you are willing to become skilled at managing your wealth. We share this with you so that you can get a real sense of just how powerful it is for you to upgrade your W.O.S. In fact, that's exactly what we'll be doing in the next several chapters—walking you through, step-by-step, the five steps to upgrade your W.O.S.

When we're done, you'll have made a fundamental shift in how you think about money and wealth that will literally make a huge impact in your financial life.

Morgan Smith, the highly successful owner and founder of Morgan Financial, talks about having over 100 things on his to do list every day. That was four years ago. Now, he has just three at a time. But, because his W.O.S. is bigger, these three things are much bigger. A typical week might include meeting with a large private investor, putting a customer service campaign in place, and acquiring another mortgage company. Then, it's off to have fun with his friends. His W.O.S. has allowed him to look at his business in an entirely different way.

In a way, it's not fair. The people who need the money the most have to work the hardest to earn it. But, in another way, it is incredibly fair because anyone, and we do mean anyone, can upgrade his or her W.O.S. and start enjoying wealth and freedom.

The real leverage point when it comes to earning money isn't acquiring more specialized knowledge about your business or investing niche. The biggest leverage point is to *first* focus on upgrading your W.O.S., and then any new software you layer on top of that will produce magnified and lasting results for you and your wealth.

In effect, your W.O.S. is the foundation upon which all your later wealth is built. If your foundation is strong, your wealth will endure and multiply. If the foundation is weak and unstable, then not only will building wealth be extremely difficult, but any wealth you are able to acquire will be at great risk of coming crashing down.

This happens all too often around the world. For example, Dennis

Pearne, author of *The Challenges of Wealth*, tells the story of one of his clients who was a software developer who had a wildly successful IPO and netted $24 million overnight. Within a matter of months, his life was a mess, and he had lost every dime. A number of emotional factors in his life surfaced, such as insecurity, shame, and even paranoia. His inner voice went quiet, and it seemed that he did everything he could to get rid of the money as fast as possible.

Maui Millionaires know that the single greatest leverage point in their wealth building is to consistently upgrade their W.O.S.

Why Your W.O.S. Determines Your Financial Success

Your brain is an amazing creation. When focused and harnessed, it can literally turn sand into gold. Don't believe us? Well, what do you call the microprocessor that runs your computer? It's made out of sand (aka silicon), and that technology literally has added trillions of dollars of wealth into the world's economy.

We live in an abundant world, where opportunity and possibility are all around us. It's your W.O.S. that makes it possible for you to see these opportunities in the sea of possibility we live in.

Did you know it is possible for people to literally starve to death just inches away from an abundance of food and nourishment? The same is true of opportunities. If your W.O.S. hasn't been conditioned to see wealth, and the ability to have it, you will pass by it every day.

Diane's Story

Why I Had to Stop Working So I Could Make Money

I started out my career as a traditional CPA with a tax practice for business owners and real estate investors. I saw what my clients did to make money and the things they did to lose it.

One of the things I learned was that there was huge opportunity in real estate, so I decided to start looking for a great deal. Every day, I drove by a small multifamily property with four units in front and two in back. The property was in great shape, but because it was more than four units, I knew I would need to come up with 25 percent or more in a down payment. It didn't matter that the property would cash flow from Day 1 even if you were able to find a loan for 100 percent of the purchase price. I knew I couldn't find that kind of loan, and I simply didn't have enough cash for the down payment on a conventional loan. So like many of the other people in the area, I just drove past.

About three months later a "sold" sign went up. I was really amazed to find out one of my clients, who didn't even have a job, had bought the property. I knew his finances and knew he didn't have the cash for the big down payment. I called this client up and asked him how he'd been able to swing it. He chuckled a little and told me that he had simply talked to the seller. She was elderly and anxious to sell, so she was happy to provide part of the financing herself so he could buy the property. He got the property for zero down. He began getting a positive cash flow of $2,500 per month immediately on the property. That positive cash flow was what was left after he'd paid all expenses on the property.

He kept the property for about a year and then sold it for a profit of about $300,000.

I drove past the property every single day and never saw the real opportunity that was right there. I was too busy working to make any real money. I learned the importance of seeing the opportunity that was there by conditioning my W.O.S. to spot the deals that are everywhere.

We live in a world of such opportunity, but 99 percent of the world is conditioned to not see these opportunities. Can your conditioning, cultural and personal, really be so strong that it would actually determine how you see the reality around you? Well, for Kelly and Rob it meant looking at their principal residence. They sat back and watched other people get rich because they didn't have the cash to get going. Yet, they were sitting on over a hundred thousand dollars in equity that they could easily access by refinancing their home. After just over two years, they were able to look back and see how they had transformed that little pot of gold into a million dollars. But, it started with first being able to clearly see what they already had.

Or consider the story of Steve. When Steve came to his first Maui Mastermind, he had a very respectable net worth of $2,000,000, but since he only invested in the stock market, that net worth didn't generate much cash flow for him. He had been able to build up a big lump of cash, but hadn't yet been able to get that money to work for him. Through his active participation in Maui and with the Maui community, he learned a different way of investing the money he already had, and in less than two years was not only able to double his net worth, but was also able to increase his passive cash flow by over 1,000 percent!

What Kelly and Rob, and Steve, and the other top 1 percent of wealth builders have come to understand is that there is never a shortage of opportunity, only a limited amount of energy with which to pursue and capitalize on those opportunities.

What do you think is one of the most common complaints of the world's top entrepreneurs and business builders? It is simply this: They don't have enough time, energy, and attention to build and create all the dreams, plans, and ideas they have in their head. In fact, they daily have a flow of ideas, any one of which could easily be a multimillion dollar or billion dollar business or investment opportunity.

When you are building wealth, you can literally train yourself to see ideas and possibilities simply by consistently making demands upon yourself to come up with creative ideas, and also by noticing all the powerful ways clever thinkers have found to turn simple ideas into great fortunes. Whether it be through synergistic mastermind sessions of a peer group of other big thinkers, or solitary brainstorming on a simple sheet of paper, when you consistently ask yourself breakthrough questions, and learn to listen for and trust the answers, you can and will train yourself to become a Maui Millionaire thinker.

What is the most important requirement for you to tap into the abundance and opportunity that we literally swim in every day? Simple. It's for you to believe it's possible. Your belief is the key that lets you access the possibility and opportunity that surrounds us. If you don't believe, then it's as if the wealth of ideas and opportunities just doesn't exist. There are practical steps you can take to upgrade your W.O.S., so that your wealth belief level shoots through the roof, and we'll cover these steps in the next few chapters, but for the moment the key point for you is this. It's easy for Maui Millionaires to make money so quickly and easily because they have trained and conditioned and upgraded their W.O.S. to the point that they see an abundance of ideas and opportunities from which to build and create great wealth. The best part is that this same wealth is waiting for you, even if it is something in your past you were never able to manifest, if you just follow the action steps we'll be presenting.

Take the example of John, a young real estate investor who came to Maui several times. For two years before John came to Maui he had been talking and talking about how much he wanted to move up from buying single-family houses to buying multiunit buildings. He had tried with no success for two years to buy larger properties. Well, within three months of getting home from Maui that first year, John had successfully and quite profitably purchased three apartment buildings! How was this possible? Did the real estate market suddenly spit up three deals that never were available before? No. It wasn't the real estate market that was different. It was John that was different. John had upgraded his W.O.S. at Maui to the point that he had a new mental picture of himself as someone able to invest in multiunit buildings. And the rest of his W.O.S. was perfectly aligned with this new image of himself.

Less than ten years ago, John worked installing carpet earning $35,000 a year. Today, he earns many times more than that as a Maui Millionaire, and he has a degree of freedom and control over his life that a decade ago he never imagined possible. The same outcome is possible for you, if only you do the work to upgrade your W.O.S.

So what really determines the wealth you enjoy? Why, you do! There are three aspects of your ability to let wealth come into your life that are controlled by your W.O.S.

First, there is your container to gather, collect, and hold the wealth that comes to you. May we let you in on a little-known secret? *You* are the container for your wealth! The bigger you become as a person, the more wealth you can hold. The bigger and more comfortable your W.O.S. becomes about wealth, the more wealth you will be able to attract into your life. Some people live their lives holding just a small thimble to gather wealth, and they wonder why they aren't wealthy. Other people who live middle-class lives have a 16-ounce glass to hold their wealth. Still others have the 128-ounce Super-Duper–sized Big Gulp to hold all their wealth. And in our world, there are a few people who have a whole swimming pool in which to hold their wealth.

How big is your wealth container? When it comes to your money, what amounts of money are you comfortable earning? What amounts are you comfortable investing? What size is your wealth container?

David's Story

When I first got started in business, I had problems asking for money for my services. It wasn't about the quality or value of what I provided, it was that my W.O.S. simply held me back. I was terrified of money. The first few checks I collected from clients made me nervous and uncomfortable. In fact, I remember one check for $1,400 that I received that caused me to literally start to sweat! My voice stuttered and stammered as I asked my client to hand me the check.

Over the years, I've grown more and more comfortable receiving money in my life. Whether it be a $10,000 check here, or a $50,000 check there, the amounts have grown with time.

In fact, I remember the first time I deposited a check for six figures that came from one of my businesses. My hands were shaking and sweaty and I photocopied the check for my scrapbook. It had a feeling of make believe to it. Was it really true? Was I really getting all this money? That moment stretched my W.O.S. in a big way.

But over the years I've had many more six-figure checks come my way. I still smile when I get them, but it just seems natural now that I get checks or wire transfers for those kind of amounts. But I was stretched about a year ago when I got my first seven-figure wire transfer from a business I had sold. But I guess I must be making progress because it was easier and more comfortable for me to receive this seven-figure payday than it was for me to collect that first $1,400 payment. Don't worry, I don't plan to stop here. I'm consistently growing my W.O.S. so that I can get comfortable someday with a steady flow of eight- or nine-figure checks flowing into my personal wealth container! I'm sure I'll have a blast swimming in that pool when the day comes!

Secondly, you have an internal model as to the volume and source of the total wealth available from which you get to draw your personal wealth. Most people live in a world where there is a limited amount of wealth to draw from, and that life is a constant scramble to fight for their share of that limited pie. What do you think life is like for people who have this model of the wealth available for them to draw from? It's either a constant struggle or battle, perhaps even a war, or it's just too hard, and they've already given up. If your model is one of scarcity and competition, it becomes much harder to see all the limitless possibilities that surround you. Plus, how much energy would you consume if you had to work to create wealth in that environment? And how much fun would it be to have to claw your share of wealth from other people? Yuck!

Imagine a sandwich shop owner who has a wealth model that said that we all must constantly fight for our fair share of the wealth pie. One day, this sandwich shop owner learns McDonalds and Taco Bell plan to open up restaurants in the exact same strip mall as his sandwich shop. How do you think this sandwich shop owner will feel? He might be fearful, bitter, and upset. He might go around complaining to whomever would listen about how unfair it was, and how the world was all tilted in favor of the big guys. Can you imagine what the outcome will be like for a business owner who has such a scarcity model of wealth?

Instead, imagine that you are in that same situation. The main difference is that your W.O.S. is one that takes as its given that we live in an abundant world, where there is always opportunity and wealth available that can be created out of thin air with creativity, daring, and commitment. You see your new neighbors as a welcome addition to the neighborhood. You know that they will bring in more potential customers. You understand that not only will you benefit from the increased traffic flow, but you will benefit by the comparison. After all, who wants fast food when they can have a specially-made sandwich at your gourmet sandwich shop? You even create a special program with local offices where they order and pay online and you then have their sandwiches ready for pickup so they get in and out in two minutes or less during the busy lunch time. They get fast *and* delicious *and* healthy food. We think you get the idea.

The bottom line is that if your W.O.S.'s model for the source of wealth is as a limited, scarce pie that people compete over, then you will live your life scrapping and clawing for wealth or resigned to have less than you could create. If, on the other hand, your W.O.S.'s model for wealth is one of abundance, where you can literally create value in the world through your imagination, then you will both build and enjoy greater wealth.

The third and final part of the equation is how your W.O.S. is programmed to transfer that wealth that you see (abundance or scarcity) to your container (yourself). Most people's W.O.S. is programmed to see hard work or luck as the only ways to transfer wealth from the source to their wealth container. They think it takes hard work to carry wealth from the source, bucket by bucket, to their container. (Or worse yet, spoonful by spoonful!) Or they think they have to hope for a freak rain to fill up their wealth reservoir. Little do they know that their belief that it takes hard work to make money is a key component of their current wealth results.

Wealthy people know that it takes work to be wealthy, but to be truly wealthy, any work they do needs to be designed so that someday the work is being done by other people or systems or technology. Why carry water bucket by bucket when you can instead build a pipeline to carry the wealth to you automatically, with minimal effort to maintain it?

That's why later in the book we'll be sharing with you the Maui Financial Freedom Formula (Chapter 17). You'll learn this simple formula that will make it so much easier for you to build, maintain, and enjoy wealth. But to truly take advantage of this formula, you'll need to make sure you upgrade your W.O.S. Which brings us back to . . .

What Beliefs Are
and How They Are Formed

A belief is simply a feeling of certainty that a particular state of affairs in the world is true. The greater that degree of certainty, the stronger that belief is said to be held by an individual.

In fact, beliefs fall into a spectrum of intensity. On the weakest end of the spectrum, you have speculation. This is something we merely posit to be true but have no real attachment to. One way to think about it is to imagine speculation as a thread holding what you speculate being true to you. A single thread is easy to break, just as it's easy for us to accept when something we speculate on turns out to be false. If this happens, we let go of the speculation by snapping the thread.

Next we have opinions. Our opinions have more power over us than mere speculation because of the ownership we ascribe to them. We say that they are ours. As you can see, a fundamental shift is taking place. Opinions are a little stronger, like twine. When you pull on them they resist being broken, but with enough force or with a sharp tug, most of us are willing to accept that an opinion we hold needs to be revised, updated, or changed.

Next we have beliefs. Beliefs are tougher, like rope. It's hard to change someone's beliefs just by pulling hard. Instead, it's best to untie the belief by pulling at just the right spot or working to unravel it. Often this happens when we ask ourselves the right question.

If we hold onto a belief long enough, or if we hold a belief to be true with enough emotional intensity, it passes from a mere belief into a conviction.

A conviction is a belief that we are *committed* to being true. When you reach the level of convictions, brute strength is rarely going to help make a change. Convictions are like padlocks that hold us to what we are committed to being true. Convictions are what happens when you add intense emotions to beliefs. The only way to change convictions is to unlock the padlock that binds you to your convictions. Rarely will a person willingly change convictions without some intense emotional experience to spin, nudge, or even jar them into a different way of seeing their old conviction. And usually this shift is preceded by some earlier event or moment that opens us up to the conviction's deletion or amendment.

And, finally, there are some beliefs that are so taken for granted that they are invisible to us. We call these beliefs givens. A given is a belief that you hold that is so basic to your belief system that it is taken for granted and operates at the unconscious level. Usually givens come to be givens by being a conviction that is held by a social group with which you identify yourself. These are the things that are socially accepted to such a degree that they become invisible. That's where the power of these givens lie, in the illusion that they don't even exist. Imagine as a young child you are allowed to go into a room to play but are told the door is being locked. Over time, you grow up living in that one room thinking that the door is locked. As an adult, you forget all about the door even existing because it's always been locked. That's the power our givens have to keep us living in a certain way. What we don't realize is that the door was never locked, and all it takes is a new model, a shift of context, to fling the door open and step into the boundless space beyond.

Why does all this matter? Because all of us have wealth beliefs at various levels, and these wealth beliefs directly and indirectly impact our ability to earn, maintain, and enjoy wealth. To change and upgrade your W.O.S. you need to understand how beliefs work.

Also, the real leverage points of your W.O.S. tend to be at the level of your convictions and givens, and not at the level of your beliefs. Usually, your wealth beliefs are just window dressing—rationalizations— for how your convictions and givens shape you. Understanding this, it's imperative for you to understand how convictions and givens are formed, so that you can take conscious control over your own W.O.S.

There are two main ways beliefs shift from being an opinion to becoming a belief or a belief becoming a conviction. The first is from the number of references or experiences we have that show that belief to be true. For example, if you have an opinion that it takes money to make money, and you then meet a rich person who inherited a lot of money, and used this money to invest and make more money, you may make this experience into a reference for the belief that it takes money to make money.* Each experience that you have that you make into a reference for that belief, in effect, is like a leg propping up the belief. Now, just as 10 legs supporting a specific belief gives it a strong base, so can one or two experiences that are of enough emotional intensity that they are thick enough and strong enough to be the support for that belief all by themselves.

When you have enough supports for an opinion, that opinion turns into a belief. But, and this is a critical point, it usually takes more than quantity to go from belief to conviction. It takes quality—in this case the emotional intensity of the experience—to go from belief to conviction.

For example, you may read about a dozen millionaires who gave money to charity and generate the belief that many wealthy people share. But imagine the power of sitting down in a room and masterminding with several Maui Millionaires who are committed to creating positive change in the world through their giving. That experience may be so intense emotionally that your belief that wealthy people share and do good in the world would become an absolute conviction of yours. The critical ingredient in this important jump is emotion.

Another key point is that most convictions are created by one-trial learning. This means you have an experience of such emotional intensity that you immediately change your behavior and beliefs in accordance with that experience to either make it more likely that you'll be able to repeat some positive reinforcement, or, more likely, to forever avoid some painful consequence you have linked up to that experience.

Maybe you were a kid and you asked your parents for money, and they got very angry at you. As a kid, you didn't realize that they might have felt uncomfortable or embarrassed or even ashamed that they didn't have the money to give you. Or maybe they felt that if they gave you the money and encouraged you in future asking that you'd become spoiled. In any case, if it was a painful enough experience you might have made the association that you shouldn't ask people for money—that asking people for money is painful. From that one experience, you took away the lesson that you never wanted to put yourself in a place where you had to ask other people for money again. This is the way convictions are formed.

Just as it takes emotion to jump from belief to conviction, it takes other

---

*It's important to note that your interpretation of what that event means, also known as the story you tell yourself about what happened, is self-created. And any event can be made to mean an unlimited number of things and thus support an unlimited number of interpretations. How powerful it is to go back and reinterpret the seminal events of our life to create more empowering meanings! If you're going to tell a story, why not make it an empowering, inspirational one that enriches your life!

people to help you turn a belief or conviction into a given. The way a given is formed is through the social lens of how a group unconsciously agrees to view the world.

When you upgrade your W.O.S., you will literally explode your income-producing power, not to mention your ability to enjoy and grow your new wealth over time. In fact, you just might say that your W.O.S. is the true magic bullet to create wealth. We are smiling as we write this because knowing this secret and actually using it are two wholly different things.

For example, how many of us know that we should exercise at least three times a week, yet still never seem to get to the gym? It's not enough to get it intellectually, you've got to get it in your gut.

Richard's Story

Richard is a graduate of three Maui Mastermind events. Like some of the other participants, while he was a millionaire before he went—he became a Maui Millionaire after the first Maui experience.

Richard had a Ph.D. and had worked at very high-level jobs in microelectronics. But he had also experienced the ups and downs of the microelectronic industry and been laid off a number of times. His family life suffered as well from his frequent absences.

Richard knew a lot about math, more than most people. He was highly educated in a growing industry, but he never could get ahead. He had to take action first before he could reap the benefits.

For Richard, that meant leaving his high-paying job and investing in real estate. It was hard to make that choice, but once he did there was no looking back. He started by investing in himself. He bought and read every book he could get his hands on about real estate. He went to numerous investment workshops. He got out into the market looking at potential deals. Today, Richard has a net worth of well over $6 million and doesn't have to worry about ever being laid off. But it all started with his willingness to take the leap to follow his passion, and with the daily effort to grow his capacity to succeed in that passion.

Knowing how to do something and actually doing something are two different things. It takes action to reap the benefits of the knowledge.

Let's try a little experiment here. Think back to when you were a young kid. What is one of your most vivid and painful experiences around the topic of money and rich people? Get clear on the memory of that experience. What did your young mind make that experience mean? Not what did it mean, but rather, what did your young, inexperienced, naive, impressionable mind make that mean to you? What lesson did you learn from that experience? Did you learn that rich people are bad? Or that you were poor? Or that you were powerless to get money, and when you tried, it led to pain?

Step back and look at your whole life. Where else do you notice that this "lesson" that you learned at such a young age influenced your later decisions, actions, or relationships?

Now imagine you are in a movie theater watching a movie of that scene of your life, but this time, imagine you are watching as the adult you of today is in that scene like a guardian angel by the side of the young you who is going through that experience. Now watch the event unfold as you watch the movie of your adult self—there to sit with, comfort, and help that young you make sense of that experience.

What words did the adult you use to comfort the young you? What wisdom or insight did your adult self share? So what did that experience really mean? How can you take this new, fresh, empowering meaning forward in your life?

Congratulations! You just had a powerful experience of one way to impact your W.O.S. It's a technique we call a "timeline reframe," and, in essence, what it does is to help you heal a past wealth wound you experienced as a child simply because you just didn't have the resources that you do now as an adult. As an aside, you can use this pattern to heal many past hurts that you "suffered" as a young child. The reason this technique is so powerful is that we all make decisions about who we are and the way the world is at a very young age. But at that time we are too inexperienced and undeveloped to make fully informed and empowering meaning out of many intense experiences. So, sadly, many of us live our lives inside the stories we created for ourselves when we were small children.

But now we are adults, with vast resources and power that we never had as kids. That's why it is so powerful to consciously recreate the stories of our past so that we live out of a tremendously more empowering meaning and story.

Remember, the only thing that really stops you from having what matters most to you is your own story of why you can't have it.

Now that you've had an experiential taste of what it's like to upgrade your W.O.S., let's get into it in greater detail. That's what we are going to focus on right now in this section of the book—how to quickly and easily start the process of upgrading your W.O.S. Notice we say "start" the process. Upgrading your W.O.S. is a lifelong process. Personally, we're grateful for this fact because it means that we don't ever have to stop learning and growing as people.

David's Story

I remember when I first got my start in business. I invested $3,400 to launch a health and nutrition company when I was 22 years old and it flopped! But I learned so much. In fact, it was at this point that I began the process of upgrading my W.O.S. At first, I took the slow route of doing this in isolation—just reading books and thinking. Over the next four years, I started to earn more money, but still I was just scraping by financially. It was at age 26 that I finally got how important it was to tap into the power of a peer group of people wealthier than I was, and I formed my first mastermind group. From there, it all happened so fast. Within six years, I was a millionaire, within seven I was a multimillionaire. But I'm still a work in progress. My current W.O.S. is set for earning millions, and I am working to upgrade it to effortlessly earn tens and hundreds of millions. Why? Because in order to do this I must grow as a person, and I love this spark to grow and learn. It keeps me excited and energized. Ultimately, for me, I know that the more I earn the more I will be able to share and contribute.

CHAPTER 3

The Five Steps to Upgrade Your Wealth Operating System

Throughout this book, you'll notice a pattern. First, we'll share a wealth concept with you, then we'll share examples of what it will mean to you if you apply it and how other people have done it to increase their wealth. Finally, we'll take you by the hand and actually do the steps necessary to apply the wealth strategy.

You have two choices about how you want to do this book. Option One is for you to just read through the book, oohing and ahing about all the wonderful ideas, but letting none of them really touch you.

Option Two is for you to engage this book. Grip it, wrestle with it, play with it, and dive deep into it. If you choose this option, you'll take the action steps with us as you progress through the book. You'll question and ponder and pounce on the ideas we share. And, as a result, you'll become much wealthier.

Ultimately, the only way for you to truly become wealthy is to do the work we'll share with you in this book. Ideas without action are simply ink on pages. *You* are the magic ingredient that injects life and reality into the pages of this book.

When you are faced with the choice to actively do one of the exercises or action steps, you can choose Option One and cop out, making all the standard excuses that poor and middle-class people make about being too busy, or needing to relax, or how you'll do it later. And, if you choose this option, you're in for an entertaining read, but that's as far as it will go.

If on the other hand, you choose Option Two, and actively participate in this book as you go, then this book, combined with the energy you breathe into it, will open up a world of wealth and opportunity for you.

Remember, the way you do anything is the way you do everything. The way you do this book is the way you do your life. If you make excuses or procrastinate, that's how you live your life. If, on the other hand, you dive into the experience of the book, not knowing exactly where it will take you, or how it will impact you, then you will be affirming a new pattern—a wealthier way of being in the world. And, this will lead you to riches as assuredly as any investment plan or business model. In fact, every Maui Millionaire started building wealth at exactly this point of departure—faced with these two options and the autonomous choice about which path they wanted to take. We hope you join us on the road to wealth as we get started with the practical steps to upgrading your W.O.S.

The Five Steps Action Plan to Upgrade Your *Wealth Operating System*

There are five steps for you to follow to upgrade your W.O.S. (Later on in this book we'll share with you a powerful secret that will let you do much of this upgrading automatically, but more on that later.)

Step One: Identify your current W.O.S.

Step Two: Pinpoint your current limiting wealth beliefs

Step Three: Delete your limiting wealth beliefs

Step Four: Install new "upgrades" to take the place of the deleted wealth beliefs

Step Five: Reinforce and condition in these upgrades over time

In the next five chapters, we'll carefully walk through each of these five steps together, so that in the end you'll have one of the most powerful wealth-creation technologies on your side, harnessed to help make you wealthy.

CHAPTER 4

Step One:
Identify Your Current W.O.S.

There are a variety of ways to uncover the coding of your current W.O.S. In the next few pages, we'll take you through four of the most powerful ways to quickly assess the status of your current W.O.S. But first, we want you to understand why it's so important to get a clear understanding of what your current W.O.S. is set for. Think about your W.O.S. like a thermostat that is set for a certain level of financial warmth and comfort. Most people live in a room with a thermostat that's set too low, and spend their lives shivering and blaming causes outside themselves for their discomfort. They blame the weather, their family, their employer, or any of a hundred reasons why they are so cold.

If only they understood that at any moment they had the power and freedom to get up and turn their wealth thermostat to any temperature they wanted!

While it was true that the way all of us have our W.O.S. created in the first place is from the outside influences we have growing up, and that as a child growing up we have very little or no control over that W.O.S., as adults we are given a powerful gift—the gift of choice.

Imagine if you could hang out with Oprah, or Donald Trump, or Bill Gates for a few days. Do you think you would learn something valuable about wealth? What if you could spend five concentrated days with them and their personal peer group of wealth stars? Do you see how this would quickly and fundamentally stretch your W.O.S. in such a way that you couldn't help but profit from the experience?

It's exactly this reason that most of our Maui Millionaires come back to Maui year after year. At first it's about themselves—to help themselves learn to build wealth. Later it becomes more about the fun and excitement with their peers. And finally it becomes a way to give back and share the gifts of Maui with the next generation of Maui Millionaires because they know that by sharing this way they not only will be able to motivate themselves, but will also be able to leverage their positive impact on the world in ways that bless so many people.

If we choose to let our W.O.S. remain in the background, running below our conscious attention, if we choose to put all the responsibility and power for our W.O.S. onto other people or institutions, we are also choosing to give up all our authentic power to create positive change. We can only change what we have the power to change. If you give that power over to some third party you are also giving up on the life you were meant to live. We are not saying it is easy to claim this power for yourself. It's not. For many people who have lived lives of financial struggle and impoverished opportunities up until this moment, this can be one of the most frightening of moments. But it's essential. And the first step is moving our current W.O.S. to the level of conscious awareness.

George's Story

George Soros, the successful founder of Soros Fund Management LLC, is a noted philanthropist as well. He typifies the true Maui Millionaire spirit. He sees a problem with how the world operates, and he chooses to do something about it, not merely sit back and complain.

He was born in Hungary in 1930 and barely survived the Nazi occupation of Budapest to undergo even more deprivations under communist rule. He left—a poor emigrant from a country with very little freedom or opportunities. He went on to accumulate a large fortune through international investments.

(continued)

George's Story *(continued)*

That's when he put his attention on the needs of the world. Perhaps, since he had experienced personally the problems of poverty and social injustice in his early life, this was his inspiration to create his foundation, Open Society Institute (OSI). OSI is dedicated to shaping public policy to promote democratic governance, human rights, and economic, legal, and social reform. On a local level, OSI implements a range of initiatives to support the rule of law, education, public health, and independent media. At the same time, OSI works to build alliances across borders and continents on issues such as combating corruption and other abuses.

He didn't like the way the world worked, and so he decided to work toward changing it.

Here are some others who went on from humble beginnings to creating fortunes and they did it in a spirit of benefiting the world.

Oprah Winfrey

Warren Buffett

Bill and Melinda Gates

Andrew Carnegie

Gordon and Betty Moore (founder of Intel and father of Moore's Law)

Michael and Susan Dell

Jeff Skoll (eBay)

Pierre Omidyar (eBay)

Okay, enough talk, time to get to work on upgrading your W.O.S.*

---

*To make it even easier for you to accurately identify your current W.O.S., we've designed a proprietary downloadable version called the Wealth Factor Test™ that you can access for free so that in 10 minutes or less you'll know what your current W.O.S. is set for. For immediate access just go to **www.MauiMillionaireBook.com**.

Exercise One: Free Association

Below you have several sentence-completion exercises.

   To really get the most out of them, simply read each sentence out loud, and quickly fill in the blank with whatever word or words pop into your mind. Don't think, don't filter, don't delay. Just read the sentence fragment out loud and fill in the blank to complete the sentence. Go!

Money is _____.

Money is _____.

Money is _____.

Money is _____.

Money is _____.

Rich people are _____.

Rich people are _____.

Rich people are _____.

Rich people are _____.

Rich people are _____.

When I'm in line to buy something, I feel _____.

When I'm in line to buy something, I feel _____.

When I'm in line to buy something, I feel _____.

When I'm in line to buy something, I feel _____.

When I'm in line to buy something, I feel _____.

When my spouse or significant other is in line to buy something, I feel

_____.

When my spouse or significant other is in line to buy something, I feel

_____.

When my spouse or significant other is in line to buy something, I feel

_____.

When my spouse or significant other is in line to buy something, I feel

_____.

When my spouse or significant other is in line to buy something, I feel

_____.

Now review your answers. How many associations were positive? How many were negative? How many were neutral? What did your answers reveal about your convictions and givens in the area of wealth and money?

_____

_____

_____

Exercise Two: Reviewing Your Past Money Inputs

One of the strongest sources of how you formed your current W.O.S. was all the programming you received about wealth and money growing up. This exercise is designed to lay out on the table for closer examination some of the most powerful wealth inputs you received as a young child. These inputs came from your family, from your community, from school, and from the dense media messages that surrounded you as you were developing into adulthood.

When you were young, what do you remember hearing about money, rich people, and wealth?

_____

_____

_____

What expressions or statements do you remember hearing when your family or other important role models or peers talked about money, rich people, and wealth?

_____

_____

_____

Kathleen was one of nine kids. Her family had some frugality around money, but generally she was told she could do anything. Yet her mother still held on to some of the survival techniques she'd learned in the Depression. She didn't like to take chances. The safest thing possible, in her opinion, was getting a job.

It was simply too risky to try to get rich. Kathleen had already made progress on her limiting beliefs before Maui, and after attending Maui was able to take it to another level. It all started for Kathleen when she first recognized what she had absorbed from her family about wealth.

What did you observe while you were growing up about how your family or other important role models felt about money, rich people, and wealth?

_____

_____

_____

Diane's Story

My parents had radically different opinions about money. My mother felt that you had to always save and that there was never enough money. My father, on the other hand, felt that you could always find another opportunity to provide the money to get what you wanted.

I can remember my father buying a Mom and Pop grocery store in Idleyld Park, Oregon (just try finding that on a map!) when I was in eighth grade. My mother was terrified about the commitment. My parents, my younger sister and I moved into a small two-bedroom house, and my mother said we needed to be happy with that because it would be a long time before we made any money. My mother was finishing out her teaching contract in Canyonville, Oregon, and so we stayed there a little longer while my father moved into the small house. Imagine my surprise when we went to visit one weekend, just a few weeks after the purchase, to see a huge two-story addition being added to our small new home before we had even moved in.

It reminded me of other times when my mother said there wouldn't be enough, and there somehow was always more than we expected.

Perhaps the saddest part of this story is that after my father's death, my mother suddenly felt poor, and acted poor. She sold their nice home and moved into a tiny one, denying herself most luxuries. She refused any offers of help, even when my husband and I offered to buy a nicer house and give her a life estate in it. (A life estate means that she could live there, free of charge, for the rest of her life.) Her reply was "I can't afford that."

I've seen echoes of both behaviors in my life. I've had to fight against the feeling of "I can't afford that" and I've consciously had to change that statement into a question, "How can I afford that?" In this way, I've upgraded my W.O.S. to accept more opportunities in my life. The consequences of a small W.O.S. are just too painful for me to accept for myself, my husband, and our son David.

While you were growing up, how did it feel in your family when the topic of money, rich people, and wealth came up? Did people get excited and joyous? Or did they get bitter and resentful? Or maybe it was such a scary and taboo topic that it was never even discussed?

What do you remember feeling about money, rich people, and wealth when you were growing up?

_____

_____

_____

David's Story

When my parents were divorced, there was real tension between my mom and dad over money. As a child, I didn't understand that this was just part of the pain and anger they both felt over a marriage that didn't work. I simply felt all that tension that surrounded the subject of money and buying things. I can remember all the times my mom would ask me to get my dad to buy me something and how my dad would only want to buy me things when I was with him, so that I would know that they came from him. As an adult, I can understand how little of this had to do with money; rather, it was simply two people hurting, scared, angry, and in need of time to heal from a painful divorce. But as a kid, the beliefs about money that I interpreted this all to mean was that it is wrong or painful to ask other people for money, and that gifts are given with strings attached, so the best way to be free of those strings is to not let other people give you things. As you can imagine, this kind of negative wealth programming made it very difficult for me to build any wealth.

One of my most painful memories of money was of a time when I was a preteen. My parents were just in the starting phase of their divorce. I was sitting in the kitchen when my mom came up to me and asked me if I knew whether or not my dad had sent the alimony and child support check yet that month, because it was late. She was clearly very distraught, and I remember how uncomfortable I felt at that moment, like I wanted to disappear. The "lesson" I learned was that money was something you shouldn't talk about. It wasn't a safe topic. It was dangerous.

(continued)

David's Story *(continued)*

As you can imagine, this lesson influenced my life in many ways. I avoided the topic of money wherever I could, and I distanced myself from money. To me it was bad and dangerous. I know to many people this might seem crazy to make one experience mean this much, but remember, I was a 12-year-old kid who didn't have the capacity at that moment to see that my mom was really in pain and needed to garner me as an emotional ally. I am not making any judgment about my parents who were and are loving, caring people who did the very best they could at a tough time in their lives, only that as a young kid I made that moment mean something that had long-term impact on my life.

I remember that I had to practice how to ask for money in front of a mirror so that when I met with clients I could stammer out my request for payment. (Thankfully this is something that now comes very easily for me.) Our early experiences about money and finances leave lasting impressions on our W.O.S., and it is critical to separate out these beliefs so that we can look at them in the light of adulthood and consciously decide if they really support the person we want to be.

Exercise Three: Reviewing Your Habitual Language Patterns

We reveal our internal thinking patterns and belief systems through the language we habitually use, especially the language we use in our own minds as we think about the world around us. The challenge is that most of us aren't aware of what our habitual language patterns are, nor what they might teach us about our current W.O.S.

This exercise is designed to help you start to become aware of your current habitual language patterns.

Part A

Are you more likely to say you "must" do something or that you "want to" do something?

Are you more likely to say you "should" do something or that you "get to" do something?

Are you more likely to say you "have to" do something or that you "choose to" do something?

Part B

What do you hear yourself saying when the subject of money comes up in conversation?

_____

_____

What are the most frequent expressions or sayings you use when you talk about rich people?

_____

_____

Exercise Four: Taking Stock of What Your Current Wealth Results Are and Where the Trend Is Heading

Perhaps one of the most accurate indicators of what your current W.O.S. is set for in financial terms is to look closely at your current financial results and which way your wealth is trending.

Looking honestly at your current wealth results, what do you think your current W.O.S. is programmed for in terms of annual income? How about in terms of net worth? Where is the trend heading, and how fast is it moving there?

_____

_____

What do you think this reveals about your current W.O.S.—being totally honest?

_____

_____

CHAPTER 5

Step Two: Pinpoint Your Current Limiting Wealth Beliefs

Remember, a belief is merely a feeling of certainty that some state of affairs is true and accurate. There is nothing in a belief that makes that belief true or false independent of how you feel about it. In fact, many of the beliefs we hold turn out to be false in the world. It's time to pinpoint with clarity and precision the negative and limiting wealth beliefs that you hold that in turn hold you back financially.

Diane's Story

Although my father was always successful at making money whenever he wanted it, the way he made the money wasn't that successful at making a life. My dad gave up everything—family, recreation, physical health—to make money.

As a result, he had his first heart attack by age 40, and by age 47 he had to retire due to health reasons. I started out following his strategy for making money by working really hard in my first business, a CPA firm located in Reno, Nevada. I only lasted five years in the business before I had to sell, simply because I was so exhausted.

(continued)

Diane's Story *(continued)*

The problem with having the belief that you have to work hard to make money is that you will forever limit how much you can make. And, while you may become a millionaire with the "start a business, work hard" theory, you'll never be a Maui Millionaire with the time, health, and relationships to enjoy the life you've created!

Exercise

Take 60 seconds for each of the following questions and quickly list out as many answers as come to mind.

My greatest worries, concerns, and fears regarding money and wealth are?

_____

_____

_____

Some of the negatives or possible negatives about being rich, or going through the process of becoming rich are?

_____

_____

_____

The reasons I can't or may not become extremely wealthy are?

_____

_____

_____

The biggest obstacles to my being wealthy are?

_____

_____

_____

Now look back at your answers to the above questions. Circle the two limiting wealth beliefs that you think more than any of the others do the most harm to your wealth building. In other words, which are the two specific limiting wealth beliefs that would make the biggest, positive difference to your wealth building if you were to change them? Write these two limiting beliefs down in the spaces below.

Limiting Wealth Belief One_____

_____

_____

Limiting Wealth Belief Two _____

_____

_____

Insider Tip: To really put your finger on your negative, limiting wealth beliefs, remember that at the time you accepted them as true you were probably very young. Therefore, the language you used was the language of a kid. For example, you may have written down that one of your limiting wealth beliefs was that "I don't have the right type of education to make money." This is grownup language, and it's not the emotionally potent language you internalized as a child.

To really be free of these limiting beliefs, you need to tap into the raw power of the emotionalized *youthful* versions of these limiting wealth beliefs. That might mean that your real limiting wealth belief wasn't that you don't have the right type of education (too sophisticated for a young child) but that instead, "I'm not enough." Or maybe that wasn't it but rather "I'm too dumb."

How do you know when you've got the language right? When you can feel yourself reacting emotionally, in your gut—then you know you've got the language right.

Go back and tweak your two limiting beliefs until the language feels primal and emotionally-charged. The bigger the charge, the bigger the positive breakthrough when you delete the belief, as you will, coming up in the next few pages.

Morgan's Story

One of our Maui Masterminders is Morgan Smith, the founder of Morgan Financial, a mortgage brokerage company with over 150 offices. When he first started out in business, Morgan had the belief that capital was hard to get access to. As you can imagine, this belief limited his success and growth in the world of mortgage banking! Over the years, Morgan has let go of that old limiting belief and now sees how easy it is for him to gain access to large amounts of money. It's the business or investment opportunity that is the real key. For example, this past year he supersized Morgan Financial's growth strategy. Previous to this time, he had grown his company by recruiting talented sales people one at a time. But this year, for the first time, he leveraged his growth by working with an investment bank to raise $100 million, to use to buy other existing mortgage brokerage businesses. Rather than recruit talent one person at a time (which they will still do), they will supersize this to acquire whole networks and teams of talent by buying new companies and adding them to the Morgan Financial family. He projects that this year they will jump to $5 *billion* in gross business volume with this new strategy. Truly, the only thing that limits any of us is the size of our thinking.

Over the years, we've observed a handful of limiting wealth beliefs that play out over and over in the lives of would-be wealth seekers. We call these 12 most damaging negative wealth beliefs the "Dirty Dozen."

The Dirty Dozen: The 12 Most Damaging Negative Wealth Beliefs

1. It takes money to make money, and I don't have any.
2. I'm poor, always was, and always will be.
3. I'm middle class, always was, and always will be.
4. It takes too much time and effort to be rich.
5. I'm just not smart enough to become rich.
6. Money is bad.
7. Rich people are low down, bad people.
8. To become rich, you have to take on huge risks.

9. People won't like me if I am rich, or worse—they'd like me only for my money.

10. It isn't possible for me to become wealthy.

11. My spouse or significant other doesn't support me enough.

12. I'm not good enough. I don't deserve it.

These are all common negative wealth beliefs and ones that the Maui Millionaires have all had to overcome on their path to wealth. You too can overcome any and all of these limiting wealth beliefs as you pursue your dreams.

Stephen's Story

One of the Maui Millionaires we interviewed for this book was Stephen, a successful business owner and investor in Colorado. But it wasn't always that way for Stephen. He grew up in a conservative household. His father was a teacher who eventually become the superintendent of schools in their community. The prevailing belief in Stephen's household was that you needed to work hard to earn a living. And the best pathway to success was through formal education, which would lead to a secure job. In essence, the feeling in his family was that the one with the most college would come out on top. And once you found that great job, you didn't dare leave it. Stephen followed this model, although it was tough going for him in college. He didn't really feel called in any direction. When he graduated, he followed in his father's footsteps and was a substitute teacher for a while.

But Stephen wanted more. He left teaching, looking for more in corporate America. After about a decade of climbing up the corporate ladder, Stephen realized that he was investing his life in building someone else's business. He and his wife Susan dreamed about building a business of their own where they could have not just the financial success, but more importantly, the time and freedom to spend with their two growing daughters.

(continued)

Stephen's Story *(continued)*

They decided that real estate was the vehicle for their wealth building. When we talked to Stephen, he shared that the single most limiting belief that stopped him in the early stages was his belief that he wouldn't be able to find the money to fund deals, even if he found them. In his mind, he kept telling himself, "I'm cash poor," and no one would ever believe in him enough to lend him the money he needed to fund good deals. This belief stayed with him for the first few years of his investing, limiting his success.

In fact, when Stephen first heard about Maui, he thought, "There's no way we could do that, not only couldn't we afford it, but they would never pick us anyway." Here's how Stephen describes what happened.

"First of all, it was such a stretch for Susan and me to even go to that first year's Maui Mastermind. I got the first e-mail talking about the event, and I knew I wanted to go, but I was sure that they would never select me to come. After I got the second announcement about the event, I couldn't stop thinking about it. I called up and asked to get on the interview list, thinking that there was no way they would choose me to come, but at least this would be a great way to find out what I'd need to do to qualify for Maui in future years. Susan and I spent an hour on the phone doing our selection interview, and at the end they picked us. I remember when we got off the phone the first thing Susan said to me was how in the world were we going to pay for this. I had no clue how we were going to pay for it, but I strongly believed that if they saw something in me and Susan that we didn't see in ourselves, then I was borrowing on their faith in us, and I trusted we would find a way. Within 30 days we sold a property and earned the money we needed to pay our way to Maui.

(continued)

Stephen's Story *(continued)*

"At the event it was like drinking out of a fire hose. All the ideas and sessions became a blur. It took me about four or five months to sort them all out and really let the lessons sink in. But when they did, I was able to make a huge shift. All my life I had believed that rich people were bad, and that I wasn't someone who could really succeed on that level. What Maui did for me was to give me permission to make a ton of money because I knew in my heart of hearts that I would be able to share and give back with this wealth in ways that fulfilled my mission to serve God. When Beverly, one of the stars there in Maui, said that it was our responsibility to make a pile of money and give it all away, it was like a switch that was flipped inside of me."

Over the next 12 months Stephen put his investing business on overdrive, closing several very lucrative transactions. The belief that it takes money to make money and that he couldn't access capital was no longer an issue for him. For example, on just one of the deals he did showing that you *don't* need money to make money, Stephen found a seasoned investor who was retiring and selling off his rental portfolio. He was firm on his price, so Stephen and Susan agreed to it if he would give them flexible terms and finance the purchase himself. They worked out a deal where the owner financed 100 percent of the purchase of a package of properties that included: 11 duplexes, 3 fourplexes, and 3 single-family homes. The total purchase price was $2.2 million with zero down and payments to be made over five years. In fact, at the closing, Stephen and Susan walked away with a check for $18,900 from the security deposits that were turned over to them! Yet we still live in a world where most people say that the reason they can't succeed financially is because it takes money to make money.

Limiting wealth beliefs seem almost crazy when we put then under the microscope, but when they operate below the surface they dramatically impact our wealth building. Take the example of Tom, a Maui Millionaire who remembers how he used to feel that he didn't have the time to focus on his investments. It was just too much energy. Sure, he had money going into his 401(k) but it was almost an afterthought.

Out of Maui, he realized that the belief he didn't have time to focus on his investments and become wealthy just wasn't true. In fact, he realized that he had all the time there was. This sparked him to take early retirement from his job, where he had worked for a number of years as a high level executive in the aerospace industry. He's loving the extra time he's created to focus on his kids and grandkids, and he's also having a blast building new businesses and investing in real estate.

In fact, this is a common theme of many Maui Millionaires. By quitting their job to focus on their passion, they are able to build wealth many times faster than when they spent their days working at a job they just weren't passionate about. (This will be discussed further in Chapter 17.)

At root, most of the negative wealth beliefs people hold trace their origins to a deeply held fear that somehow they aren't enough.

David's Story

For many years one of the driving fears that ran in the background of my life was the fear that I wasn't enough. This fear was constantly at the periphery of my consciousness, and I only felt it as this forboding sense of anxiety. For many years, I tried to fill this perceived hole in myself by succeeding, first in sports, and later in the business world. It was only when I came to terms with this hurting part of myself that I was able to let go of the frenzied chase for outward success and realize that I was enough, just the way I was. For me the upgraded belief I installed in its place was, "I am a child of God, who is, was, and always will be, deserving of great love." When I made this shift, I began to enjoy an inner peace that stays with me to this day. Now, when I am building my wealth, it isn't about filling a hole in me, but rather my wealth building has become a joyous expression of what's best inside of me and a powerful way to contribute to the world.

Let's take stock of where we are. At this point you've identified what your current W.O.S. is programmed for. You've also identified several of your limiting wealth beliefs, including writing down two of your most limiting wealth beliefs. In the next three steps, you'll learn how to hit the delete button and make these limiting beliefs disappear from your life, how to replace them with empowering new beliefs, and how to condition in these upgraded beliefs over time to sustain your change.

CHAPTER 6

Step Three: Delete Your Limiting Wealth Beliefs

Remember what your beliefs really are; they're just a feeling of certainty you have that a specific thought is true. And when you look at the hierarchy of beliefs, remember that the really limiting wealth beliefs you have will either be convictions or givens. This means that you'll have to use emotion to cut away at them.

The following four techniques are all about giving you the power to hit the delete button on your limiting beliefs and to free yourself forever of their limiting hold on you and your life.

Four Techniques to Delete Limiting Beliefs

Choose one of your two limiting beliefs to work with for the moment. You can come back and repeat these exercises with the other belief later.

Write the belief you are working with in the space below:

_____

_____

_____

Using these four techniques you'll notice that your negative wealth belief disappears bit by bit. Then, in the next chapter, you'll have the opportunity to create a new empowering replacement belief that you'll want as part of your upgraded W.O.S.

Let's begin.

Remember all a belief is is a feeling of certainty that some state of affairs is true. A belief is supported by references, and each of these references is like a leg upon which the belief rests. So let's get busy knocking out those supports so that you weaken the old, limiting belief. It's like clearing the ground for the even more powerful techniques that will follow.

Technique One: Question It!

In the space below, list all the possible things that call that limiting belief into doubt.

Isn't there even one counterexample to show that in at least one case that belief isn't true? What other examples show that that limiting belief isn't true in every case? What counterexamples or exceptions to your limiting belief exist in the world?

_____

_____

_____

_____

_____

Technique Two: Get Radical!

Take your limiting belief to the extreme, and then list why it can't be true. For example, if your limiting belief used to be "Rich people are bad," then take this to the logical extreme. Imagine what the world would look like if *every* rich person were an evil villain. It almost makes you laugh to imagine this, it is so warped. Of course, there are some rich people who are nice and generous and kind. After all, aren't there some people who started off poor and incredibly nice and good people and then later became wealthy? Did these people suddenly become horrible people once they had money? Imagine Mother Teresa were still alive and you gave her a billion dollars. Would she become a bad person? Of course not, she would use that money to help a huge number of needy people live a better life, with dignity. Now it's your turn to take that old, limiting belief to the extreme and see how out of touch it really is.

_____

_____

_____

_____

_____

Technique Three: Ridicule It!

It's been said that the most powerful way to make people unwelcome is not to get angry with them, but to laugh at them. Well, it's time to make that old, limiting belief very unwelcome. Look at your limiting belief with your most witty and satirical comic eye. What's silly about the belief? In fact, what's ridiculous about the belief? Why is it obviously wrong? What are all the references that prove that it is not only false, but absolutely false, silly, warped, or totally skewed?

For example, using the limiting belief that rich people are bad, let's poke fun at it. Santa Claus has all the toys to give to kids everywhere and owns a lot of real estate in the North Pole, is he a bad guy? If you were a charity looking to raise money, where would you go, to all the kind-hearted, loving _poor_ people? No way, you'd find those people with money and a heart. And let's get real here, how many really rich people do you know personally? Isn't it true you based this belief mostly off the "secondhand smoke" popular media portrayal of rich people? What kind of accurate reporting of rich people do you think skeptical and financially-strapped reporters are really going to make? Hmm ... let's think for a moment about that one! We hope you are getting the idea here. Now it's your turn to let loose on that out-of-fashion, old-school, limiting belief. Have at it!

_____

_____

_____

_____

_____

Congratulations! You've started the process of loosening up that old limiting belief. The problem is that these techniques are too cognitive, and they only hit the belief with logic, not emotion. Remember, the way the belief became a conviction or a given in the first place was with the addition of strong emotion. Therefore, you need to use emotion to get rid of it.

Technique Four: Get Leverage!

One of the fundamental truths about human behavior is that we are motivated to take action when we reach a threshold of pain. Sure, we might like to have a warm fire to relax by, but it's rarely that warmth and comfort that gets us into gear. Usually, it's the penetrating chill that forces us to find heat or suffer.

So it's your turn to see what that old, limiting belief is really costing you in your life. To get the most out of the following exercise, you will need to be willing to emotionally connect with the painful costs and consequences of that old, limiting belief that you want so badly to let go of. If you notice yourself dissociating from feeling during this exercise, we urge you to play full out and get back in there and really experience the full feeling and weight of how much you've lost and will continue to lose by dragging that old belief around with you. Okay, time to go for it.

Write the old limiting belief down here again:

_____

_____

_____

_____

_____

What is the price I am paying for holding onto this false and limiting belief?

_____

_____

_____

_____

_____

What is it really costing me? What experiences and opportunities have I lost out on forever by holding on to this limiting belief?

_____

_____

_____

_____

How does this make me *feel*?

_____

_____

_____

_____

How is it hurting, directly and indirectly, those people I love most? What is the impact of this limiting belief on my kids? What kind of role model am I being? How am I cheating the people I care about most out of what they really deserve from me by stubbornly refusing to let go of that old, costly, selfish belief?

_____

_____

_____

_____

How does this make me *feel*?

_____

_____

_____

_____

What will be the ultimate price I will pay if I don't change this false and limiting belief? If I stubbornly refuse to change this belief what will the ultimate consequence be?

_____

_____

_____

_____

_____

And how does this make me *feel*?

_____

_____

_____

_____

_____

Good job, you're done with this part. We know it wasn't easy, but we admire your honesty and courage. It is these same two qualities that will help you succeed and become a Maui Millionaire.

At this point, you have a belief that is tottering on the brink of the garbage bin. The final thing you need to do to tip it over the edge and be freed of this baggage forever is to consciously choose an empowering belief to take it's place. This is exactly what you'll do in the next chapter.

CHAPTER 7

Step Four:
Install Upgrades
to Your W.O.S.

Have you ever heard the phrase "nature abhors a vacuum"? Well, so does your W.O.S. Anytime you delete an old, limiting belief you need to choose a new empowering belief to take its place. This freedom to be your own programmer of your W.O.S. is one of your greatest freedoms in life.

Let's create and install your upgraded belief step-by-step.

First, choose a new, empowering belief to replace that old, limiting one you deleted in the last step. For example, if the nasty old belief was "rich people are bad," maybe you'll choose a new belief like "I use my wealth to bless people's lives" or "Money is a tool with which good people create massive joy in the world." Or maybe the old belief was "I can't be wealthy," and you are choosing instead the new truth "I can do anything I set my mind to and consistently work toward." Or, "I am a money magnet who is joyfully building my financial fortune."

Your turn . . .

My new, empowering wealth belief is _____

_____

_____

Now work through the following questions, filling in your answers in the space provided.

What was the *core positive intention* of the old belief? (e.g. "Rich people are bad" has a core positive intention of your desire to be a good person—generous, caring, and compassionate. The core positive intention is to protect you and help you live your life in alignment with your values.)

_____

_____

In what ways will this new empowering belief still satisfy the core positive intention of the old belief but do it in a way that is so much more healthy and sustainable?

_____

_____

_____

What are all the potential references that show, support, prove that this new belief is accurate, doable, possible, true?

_____

_____

_____

Now that you've committed to your new belief, what are all the wonderful benefits you get out of *living* this new belief? How will living this new belief bless your life and the lives of those you love? How will your life be forever changed, improved, moved, touched by living this new belief?

_____

_____

_____

How does this new, brighter future of limitless possibility make you feel? Are you inspired? Moved? Joyous? Write down how it makes you *feel* . . .

_____

_____

_____

There is one more part to Step 4 to finish the installation of your W.O.S. upgrade. What is one specific action step you could take in the next 72 hours that would be symbolic of you living your new empowering belief?

_____

_____

Now resolve to do it! Schedule it in your calendar immediately! Never leave the scene of a new wealth upgrade without taking a clear, definite action step to declare that belief real in your life!

In a moment, we'll walk you through the final step in your W.O.S. upgrade—reinforcing the upgrade over time. But first, we have a fun little quiz for you to take to see how well we're doing explaining the key principals of Maui Millionaires, and then you'll see the list of the 12 core wealth beliefs of Maui Millionaires.

Quick Quiz on the Key Beliefs of Maui Millionaires

1. The best investment you can make is an investment in _____.
   (yourself)
   Maui Millionaires know that you have got to invest in yourself—in your education and growth—before you can expect to reap the rewards. You always have to pay your dues!

2. Always be willing to intelligently spend money to buy _____.
   (time)
   Maui Millionaires know that their most precious resource is their time. In one very important sense, wealth isn't about money at all, it's about time. In fact, one way to measure your wealth is to see how long your wealth can support your current lifestyle without your actively working anymore. For most people in the world the answer is in days, weeks, or at most a few months. For others, the answer is 6 to 12 months. Maui Millionaires measure that answer in years or, in many cases, in generations!

   So how can you invest money to save you time? Can you hire someone to do many of the day-to-day activities that eat up your time but produce little satisfaction or financial return for you? Can you hire an expert to help you handle some key area so that you produce a fast result that is many times better than what you could have done on your own? The key is to take this saved time and reinvest it in wealth-building activities.

3. The fastest and easiest way to change your beliefs, and especially to shift and change your W.O.S., is through your _____.
   (peer group)

We're sure you've heard the old expression that if you lie down with dogs you're going to get up with fleas. Well, if you hang out and spend your life with stressed-out, negative, unhappy people who struggle to make ends meet and complain about it every step of the way but never do anything to improve their situation, then over time you'll slip further and further down this road to a painful financial end. If, on the other hand, you spend most of your time with people who are positive, committed to making their lives what they want them to be, and who believe in an abundant world, then you'll find it much easier for you to create a satisfying, fulfilling, wealthy life for yourself. We become the people our most consistent peer groups see us to be. Maui Millionaires know this, and they create a peer group to support creating real and enduring wealth in all areas of their lives.

It's interesting that most people come to Maui the first time because they want to learn how to make more money or to leverage the wealth they already have to create time freedom without sacrificing cash flow. Although they do learn this, what keeps so many of them coming back year after year is the people they meet and the friendships that grow out of Maui. One of the fastest shortcuts to wealth is to become part of a peer group of wealthy people who can support, encourage, and spark your growth.

The 12 Core Wealth Beliefs of Maui Millionaires

One: Accept full and complete responsibility for your life and everything in it.

Two: Recognize that wealth is really a state of mind—a sense of abundance, gratitude, and peace of mind.

Three: Enduring financial wealth is a result. Its cause is our internal feelings of wealth and the specific actions that we consistently get ourselves to take in building financial wealth.

Four: Money is important, very important, in our culture, but it is a blessing only when combined with the state of mind known as wealth. Money without wealth doesn't fulfill or enrich someone, although neither does the lack of money ever enrich someone.

Five: Money is a form of stored/potential energy that magnifies the person we are in the world. If we are generally happy, joyous, generous, and honest, money will allow us to do more with this part of ourselves. If we are generally negative, fearful, closed, and angry, then money will heighten these parts of us. Money itself is neutral. It is the person we are that determines the way the money is used. Money doesn't make the person; money *reveals* the person.

Six: We can literally attract money and wealth into our lives by the thoughts we think and the person we are. In fact, this is the start of all great fortunes in the world.

Seven: We live in an abundant world. There is no fixed sum of wealth. We can always expand the sum total of the wealth available through our creative powers and imagination.

Eight: We each have a responsibility to grow to become the best person we can be. And the pursuit of wealth is really a gymnasium to work on the person that we are. Don't become rich for the money, become rich for the person you will become as you stretch yourself. Understanding this, Maui Millionaires know that making money is more about the way you pursue creating wealth than the outcome. You can never separate the end of having wealth from the means you used to create that wealth.

Nine: One of the truest tests to determine if you are wealthy is to honestly observe how you feel about other people's successes. While Maui Millionaires might use other people's successes as a kick in the behind (spur) to greater effort on their part, Maui Millionaires don't feed the emotions of jealousy or envy. Maui Millionaires choose to celebrate the success of others, and in so doing subconsciously give themselves permission to celebrate their own successes too.

Ten: To be wealthy, you must grow your comfort level with doing things that scare you. Creating wealth requires you to consistently do the things that in the past might have scared you. Maui Millionaires consistently do the things they are afraid to do and learn to take action in the presence of their fears.

Eleven: The fastest, easiest way to wealth is to create a peer group of wealthy people. Over time, the social lens of how other people see us, and the infectious nature of character and beliefs within our social networks, are the easiest ways to reprogram ourselves for wealth. One of the highest leverage wealth actions you can take is to consciously build a peer group with which to mastermind as you build your wealth.

Twelve: Maui Millionaires understand that in order to be truly wealthy they need to build their financial income streams in such a way that they are passive, residual streams of income. Maui Millionaires build income streams that require very little of their personal time overseeing and that yield them cash flow year after year.

CHAPTER 8

Step Five: Reinforce and Condition in Your New *Wealth Operating System*

Congratulations on coming as far as you have. The average person is living in a financial daze and has no idea that there is such a thing as a W.O.S., let alone know what his default program is set for. Not only have you become consciously aware of your W.O.S.'s current setting, but you have taken the action steps to consciously make an upgrade through the exercises in the last four chapters.

We urge you to continue this work over your lifetime because while you have made an important shift, it is only the beginning of a lifelong process. It's not the case that you delete one limiting wealth belief and install a new upgraded empowering belief and then you instantly become fabulously wealthy. It's going to take some time pruning, weeding, and nurturing your W.O.S. for all that wealth to flow into your life. Trust us on this, though: If you put in the energy and conscious effort to continue the process of upgrading your W.O.S., the money will come—of that we are absolutely certain.

Which brings us to the final step of the five-step process: reinforcing and conditioning in your wealth upgrades over time. Let's be clear here. You've made amazing progress by making a fundamental shift in one key area of your W.O.S., but that's not enough. Over time, if you don't take the specific action steps we're about to share with you, you'll find that your W.O.S. will slip and sag back to where it was. Why? Because unless you consciously create a supportive wealth environment, the default environment in our society is one that is filled with poverty inputs.

What follows are three powerful action steps you can take to lock in the changes in your W.O.S. so that they become a powerful, *permanent* part of your new W.O.S.

Action Step One:
Identify Your New Wealth Behaviors

List your new empowering wealth belief you just installed:

_____

_____

_____

If you have fully embraced your newly upgraded, empowering wealth belief, how will you behave differently as a result of your fully living that new belief? (For instance, if your new belief is that you are deserving of great wealth and will use it in ways that bless the world, then you might be willing to set more ambitious goals in life, look for new wealth opportunities, start to notice all the good things wealthy people do for your community, or put a higher value on your time.)

_____

_____

_____

What actions, behaviors, ways of being in the world would your friends and family see? (You could hire a housekeeper once a week because your time is too valuable to spend cleaning; start a new business part-time and diligently focus on it; take financial and business workshops; be much more aware of your habitual language around money and wealth, and so forth.)

_____

_____

_____

What actions, behaviors, ways of being in the world would your work associates observe? (You could become much more focused and productive at work; ask for and expect a raise; you might see a new income opportunity for the company and present it in a cohesive business plan to your boss along with a request that you head up the new division with an equity stake; or you might simply—gulp—make a life-changing plan, so that within 24 months you could transition to being self-employed and completely finished with working for someone else ever again, and so forth.)

_____

_____

_____

What actions, behaviors, ways of being in the world would complete strangers notice about you that would be tangible expressions of your living fully consistent with your new empowering wealth belief? (They might see you volunteering for local charities; they might notice your ease around the topic of money and wealth; they might see the peace of mind you enjoy and find that a very compelling reason to get to know you, and so forth.)

_____

_____

_____

Action Step Two:
Reinforce Your Upgrade
with Immediate Action and
Build in a Layer of Accountability
to Make Your Upgrade Real

Using the ideas that you just listed, choose two specific action steps you will take in the next 72 hours that will prove to yourself that you have made this shift in your thinking and will reinforce your deep commitment to making your change last:

Commitment One _____

Commitment Two _____

Now get an accountability partner and share what you have learned about your W.O.S., including your old wealth belief and its cost to your life, your new empowering belief, and the two action commitments you will take in the next 72 hours. Ask them to support you and hold you accountable to these action steps.*

Action Step Three:
Create a Wealthy Peer Group
of Maui Millionaires or
Maui Millionaires in the Making

The most powerful way to reinforce a wealth upgrade over time is through the social lens of how other people you spend time with and identify yourself with both see you and see wealth in general. We quickly take on the belief systems, habits, and values of those people we spend the most time with. As a general rule, if you want to see what your W.O.S. is set for, look at the W.O.S. of the five people you spend the most time with in your life. Chances are that your W.O.S. is in alignment with theirs. That's why it's so critical to build a peer group of successful people.

For Maui Millionaires this means masterminding with like-minded wealth seekers who are equally committed to living a life that matters. Maui is the key that unlocks the door to tap into the power of the mastermind concept. In fact, an integral part of Maui is the proprietary technology of how to create and build with and through other people. This is the same technology that you are going to learn in this book to supercharge your wealth building and make any of your dreams real and doable. This is critical for two very important reasons.

---

*We strongly recommend that you invest in your accountability partner by buying him or her a copy of this book. Then, the two of you (or three, four, or five of you) can form a mastermind group to practice and implement the ideas, techniques, and strategies from this book into your life. We've even created some special mastermind tools for readers like you who want to get the most out of this book. For complete details of these powerful mastermind tools, just go to **www.MauiMillionaireBook.com** or see the Appendix.

First, when we dream big and look to touch the world many times our dreams are more than we can do alone. In fact, this is usually the case. We don't know enough, so we need input from other people. We don't have the time and energy to do it on our own, so we must enroll other people in our dream so that together we can build something magnificent and worthwhile. Plus we need the feedback from honest, talented, outside people, and the new, fresh ideas they put forth, and the contacts they bring to us.

The second reason we must build with and through other people goes back to something we said earlier. We said that the biggest reason to become rich is so you can become the person you must become in order to attain and maintain real wealth. Well, we are social beings. In an important way, we know ourselves only through the social dance of interacting with other people. The spirit of Maui means that we see other people as they really are—bright, shining children of God who have always been and who will always be deserving of great love and who are capable and powerful beyond their wildest dreams. We need our mastermind partners to see this inherent goodness and power and light within us, because this is one crucial key to setting it free. If we live in a world where everyone around us sees us as ordinary, we will soon live down to that stunted vision of ourselves.

The great power of Maui is that when we regularly interact with the Maui Millionaire community, we draw strength and inspiration from the positive and powerful way other people see us. And through this positive form of peer pressure, we can build and grow and enjoy and share at levels we never knew possible.

We see ourselves through the social lens of how other people see us. Their opinion is a strong force that draws us to live up to or down to their vision of us.

The best part about this is that if you can find or create the right peer group, you don't have to struggle or work hard to upgrade your wealth beliefs; it literally becomes easy and automatic. It's like an empowering form of positive peer pressure!

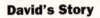

> ### David's Story
>
> One of the most important people in my life from a wealth perspective was my first mastermind and business partner for 10 years, Peter. At the time I first met him I was literally living in the attic of a garage racing to finish college before my money ran dry. I met him at a wealth workshop we were both attending. We struck up a friendship there and formed a mastermind group together. Each week, we met over the phone to support each other's dreams and hold each other accountable.
>
> Over the next several years, Peter helped me completely upgrade my W.O.S. to the point where I went from living in that garage to living in a 4,000-square foot estate home with incredible views, a 23-foot waterfall in the back yard, and a hot tub that fit 12 people! During that time, I went from a net worth of zero to being first a millionaire, and then a multimillionaire. And it all started by finding and creating a peer group of people who believed in me when I wasn't able to believe in myself.

It's your peer group that makes such a huge difference in your wealth building. This is so powerful and necessary that not only have we dedicated an entire section of this book to the power of creating a mastermind group, but we've also founded the world's premier wealth-building community based on the philosophy and spirit you are learning about in this book. For complete details about how you can become an active member of this community, make sure you read the Appendix of this book and follow the action steps it lays out to register to join for *free*! Or go to **www.MauiMillionaireBook.com** right now to register.

If you were to ask us what our role in Maui is today, we'd immediately tell you that we see ourselves as the founders and guardians of the world's premier wealth-building community, whose prime focus is on how to mastermind together to help each member create real wealth, and to share that wealth in ways that bless the world.

But let's back up for a second. In the past, from whom have you received most of your financial programming? If you're like most people, you would answer from poor and middle-class individuals. Can a poor or middle-income person help you program your W.O.S. for wealth and financial prosperity? Not likely.

Here's the good news. It is totally possible and doable to upgrade your W.O.S. Do you think we were both programmed for wealth from a young age? Hardly. We've had to work consistently to upgrade our W.O.S. in order to enjoy the freedom and financial success that has come into our lives. And you can do the same thing—only you will be able to do it faster and easier than we did. Why? Because you get to benefit from all the dead ends and painful lessons we made along the way. In *The Maui Millionaires*, you get the distillation of our collective experience of earning tens of millions of dollars and creating a lifestyle of wealth and abundance, without all the trial and error we had to go through.

We have one more reason why it is so critical for you to do what's necessary to upgrade your W.O.S.—because of the influence you have on the W.O.S. of your friends and family. If you still need one more reason to become massively wealthy, then do it for the role model of compassionate wealth and joyous abundance you'll become for your kids, your grandkids, and those people closest to you. One last benefit you get from upgrading your W.O.S., in addition to building and enjoying greater wealth—you get to share your W.O.S. and positively influence the W.O.S. of the people you care about most.

Tom and Christine's Story

Tom and Christine shared how one of the biggest blessings they've gotten out of Maui has been the positive impact they've been able to make in the W.O.S. of their kids and grandchildren. For example, they took their 13-year-old grandson with them to Hawaii. They were sitting on the beach in front of their condo (a resort rental property that they had recently purchased), explaining to him the wealth-multiplying effect of buying this property with leverage. They walked him through the result of buying the property for all cash, then with 50 percent down, then for 20 percent down, then for nothing down. Within 20 minutes, a light bulb went off for their grandson, and he understood how powerful leverage was when used properly for wealth building. Can you imagine the effect of that simple lesson?

Tom shared how his family dealt with money when he was a kid. It just wasn't talked about at all. Its presence was overwhelming by the way it invisibly occupied so much space in the room.

(continued)

Tom and Christine's Story *(continued)*

Here was their grandson who now had such a healthy reference for talking about money. And it got even better. Tom and Christine took him to meet the other multimillionaires who were members of the building's homeowners association. And when their grandson walked in the room, Tom introduced him as a "future millionaire." His grandson loved it. What a powerful yet subtle shift that Tom and Christine had started with their grandson at the level of how he saw himself.

They also shared how they recently had a family meeting where for about an hour they shared openly and candidly about the big picture of their finances and investment strategies. Their kids asked a ton of questions and really were energized to have the permission to talk about this normally culturally-taboo subject. At the end of the conversation, Tom and Christine's kids were talking about ways they could either start or upgrade their investing and financial strategies. By having the courage to share this normally out-of-bounds subject, Tom and Christine are helping to upgrade their whole family's W.O.S. This is the way that generational wealth and financial fluency and freedom are created Maui-style—by a caring family having the courage to openly talk about money in a way that affirms everyone else in the family.

PART TWO

MAUI WEALTH LEVERAGE STRATEGY TWO:
Dream Big!

CHAPTER 9

The 25 Keys to Dreaming Big

Dream no small dreams for they have no power to move the hearts of men.

—GOETHE

Everything happens because of a dream. If you're not living your dream, you're living someone else's dream.

Look at a normal life for the average person today. You get up earlier than you really want to because the alarm goes off. Rush through a workout (or wish you had time for one) and go to a job that occupies most of your waking time. The dreams of your childhood are long past. Now, it's about working, providing for a family, and maybe, someday, you'll have some time for you.

If you're working for someone else, chances are you're working on someone else's dream. Now here's the amazing part. The owner of the company might never have purposely chosen the course of his business, so it's not even his dream. His mother always had the dream that someday her son would own his own business or his high school math teacher told him he was gifted in math and needed to do something in that field. He might have married someone his family told him he should marry (through spoken or unspoken comments and actions), lived in a city and neighborhood where someone else thought he should live and work. It's a life of chance and passive coincidence. No wonder we go through midlife crises! It's our subconscious waking up and saying, *Hey wait a minute! What happened to those great dreams we had once upon a time?*

Some people decide to start their own business in hopes that this is the way to personal freedom. The entrepreneurial spasm lasts long enough to quit a job and start working for their own business. But, for most people, they run their own business exactly the way they used to work a job. The difference is that instead of just one boss, they now have a whole lot of bosses to keep happy. We call them customers or clients. The business owner still has no control and still isn't following her deepest, most precious dreams.

Ask yourself: If you have your own business, is it run exactly the way you want it to? If you work for someone else, are you living your highest purpose? Are you achieving what you wanted in your life, right now?

A big part to being a Maui Millionaire is purposely choosing the life you want to lead. Then, it's a matter of setting the game up so you get exactly what you want. If you don't choose where you're going, you'll never get there. The dream is the beginning. It's the seed and spark that grows into a life of abundance and wealth.

Rediscover Your Dreams

As a child, we had dreams. They were in the language of children because we were children. Then we put aside many of those childish dreams and "grew up." Of course, growing up meant that we followed what the adults around us said being a grown up was. We gave up on the big dreams.

Instead, we started substituting goals for dreams. If you were raised in a typical American household, those goals had to do with success and money. They focused on the outer achievements, not on inner values and dreams. It's pretty ironic that with the primary focus on those kind of achievements, more and more people find their wealth slipping away. Could it be that there is something fundamentally off with how the average person thinks about the future? Of course! And in this section of the book you'll learn how to tap back into your real passion and purpose in life as you clarify *your* big dreams.

The big dreams of a Maui Millionaire are not always brand new dreams. You're not reinventing dreams. You're rediscovering the dreams of your childhood. Now, though, you're doing it with the years of experience and education that allow you to use the language of adults, with the heart and faith of a child.

False Dreams

What stops people from becoming who they genuinely aspire to be?

- He doesn't know *who* he really is.

- She's let the process of living life crowd out her dreams.

- He has mistakenly identified his future based on past labels (shy, lonely, funny, athletic).

- She fears she is not enough, that she'll be rejected, that she'll fail, or she will be immobilized by a general anxiety of the unknown.

Dream No Small Dreams

If you're committed to going out there and pursuing a dream, make sure the dream is worthy of your time and attention. Seek the game worth playing. If your current life doesn't have a dream big enough to risk the game, then find one that does. Find a dream so juicy, so appealing, and so powerful that it compels you to work to reach it. It calls to you, sings to you, sinks its hooks into you and won't let you go. What's a dream that is so powerful that you will live part of your life for it?

In the next few chapters, we're going to look at how to rediscover the dreams you've had and then supersize them in Maui fashion to create something even bigger and bolder. We believe that you were born to do something great, and now it's time to rediscover exactly what that greatness is!

Dream Big!

Corporations pay thousands of dollars to work on articulating their company vision. The corporate vision generally isn't just about making money. It's about the deeper reasons why the business exists and the powerful passions that fuel the organization.

The same is true for us. You have a personal vision as well. Sadly, most of us don't bother to take the time and energy necessary to articulate our own vision—the dreams that make everything we do worthwhile. Without a dream to pursue, our spirit wilts and our soul shrinks.

Your big dream is your personal vision that taps into the passion you have in your life. Passion is the energy of your heart. It drives you to perform at the highest possible level. It gives you the fuel to keep going when others around you quit. Passion dares you to ask more, to do more, to be more. Passion allows you to make mistakes, get knocked down, and get up for another round. Passion is the limitless energy that allows you to achieve extraordinary results. It's the juice that makes life so sweet.

What is so important to you that you would invest part of your life going after it without any direct reward or compensation, just because you felt so powerfully moved by that dream? That's a first step in determining the dreams that aren't just merely financial. If your most compelling desire right now is to create a certain amount of money or passive cash flow, ask yourself—why? Imagine you have all the money and financial success you've ever wanted, then what? When you achieve that level of wealth, what are you going to do with the money? Who is the person you dream of being? That's how you can tap into the most compelling aspect of those dreams.

Three Ways to Rediscover Your Dreams

Sometimes finding out what our dreams actually are can be the hardest part. Here are some ideas to jump start the process.

Technique One: **Do a dream download.** Consider who would you love to be ... what would you love to do ... to have. That's your passion. Think about what you are good at. That's your talent. Reflect on what's most important to you. Those are your values. Now, what were you born to do? That's your destiny.

Take a blank piece of paper, and put it in front of you. Set a timer or ask someone to time you for 10 minutes. Pick up a pen (not a pencil!) and write. You might make a list of dreams. Or you might describe your dream life. Or perhaps you just answer the questions above. Whatever it is, keep writing. Don't stop until the timer stops.

Kerry's Story

Kerry from San Diego tells of the first of many ahas he received at his first Maui Mastermind. One of the pre-exercises was to get ready for the Come As You Will Be Party, set for five years out. Each partygoer was to come as he or she would be. For one night, you live in your future. One of the exercises Kerry was given was to create a collage of where he is now and then where he would be in five years.

He did the first collage for the current year. That went easy. But, as he went through the collage for his future in five years, he realized it was exactly the same as the current collage. That's what we call break-out thinking. It was the ah-ha that meant he'd never look at anything the same.

Kerry realized that he had the wealth he had been working toward for so many years. He'd gotten so used to just keeping his head down and only looking forward, that he hadn't stopped to marvel at how far he'd come since his days working for Qualcomm. In fact, he'd totally missed the fact that he'd already arrived!

He checked in with us three months later. Kerry had been selling his higher maintenance real estate to invest in bigger deals that needed less work. His goals were now mainly focused on fulfilling his adventure and relationship dreams. The most exciting things in his life during the last few months were (1) helping his son land his first fish and (2) going riding on ATVs in the desert with his daughter.

Maui Millionaire Tip. Clearly identify your dreams in every area of your life and seek the balance to give you everything you want.

Technique Two: **Make a dream collage.** Assemble a stack of magazines, blank poster board, a glue stick, and a pair of scissors. Cut out pictures and create a poster of your dream life. Include pictures of whatever speaks to you.

Supersize your dream collage. Get a few friends together and each work on the project individually. Each person will create a collage of his or her life today on one side of the poster board. Assemble a dream collage on the other side of the poster board that will show your life five years from now.

Work with Passion

KEY CONCEPT

The dream collage activity is a great way to start a dialogue between attendees at office and business meetings and workshops. Here's how it can work.

- Attendees start off the day by creating a today collage, describing in pictures where they are today.

- Each attendee does a brief presentation with the collage to explain who they are to the group.

- Supersize the activity by adding an ending part to the workshop with a collage that shows where they will be in five years.

- Hang them up around the office after the workshop. It's a great way to go back and remind each other of who we really are and where we want to be.

Technique Three: **Talk to Your Friends.** Chances are your friends, family, and business colleagues know things about you that you don't even know. We tend to look at ourselves through the eyes of others who have been critical of things we've done. Have you ever noticed how you remember the one bad comment you got about something you did and can't for the life of you remember the dozen good comments you received?

We're conditioned to look for the fault in ourselves. That helps us find the things we need to improve on, but it also means that we overlook the things we do well. Spend a lifetime working on your faults, and you'll live a lifetime being mediocre. Instead, look for those things that you have a talent for and that you are passionate about. Chances are the things you do well will unlock the secret of your dreams.

How can you find out what those dreams are? Your friends might hold the answer—ask them. Send them a letter or e-mail and ask for their help. Here is a sample of what that letter might say:

Sample Letter or E-mail

Dear _____,

I'm writing because I'd value your input and insight to help me get a fresh, outside perspective on what you've observed my greatest strengths, talents, and unique gifts are. I respect your clarity and judgment, and would love your thoughts and opinion.

If you're wondering where all of this comes from, well, I was reading an inspiring book recently, and it challenged me to ask the 10 people I admire most in my life to tell me what they see in me as my greatest strengths and talents, parts of me that I may just take for granted or not even see in myself.

What are the five strengths, talents, or unique gifts you see in me?

I've made a firm commitment to live more of my life out of my strengths and specialness instead of my fears or limitations.

Thank you for helping me to be more of who I really am. It's a special gift you are giving me.

Your friend,

Create Your Own Field of Dreams

Have you ever seen the movie, *Field of Dreams*, starring Kevin Costner? Remember how in that movie Costner plays a struggling Iowa corn farmer named Ray. One day Ray has a vision in a dream—to plow under a section of his corn fields and build a baseball diamond. The movie then follows Ray's journey as he pursues his "crazy" dream. Along the way, he deals with negative family pressures, financial pressures, and a whole lot of self-doubt, but he holds true to his dream. In the end, he finds not only financial success, but the chance to reconcile with his father, a reward far greater than money. The movie is an allegory that inspires and moves you to create your own field of dreams, and now is the time to do it!*

---

*Books, movies, and music are some of the most powerful tools to inspire and motivate you. Would you like to download a list of our personal all-time favorites? Then go to **www.MauiMillionaireBook.com** and you'll find the David and Diane Top Ten List of Inspirational and Educational Films, Books, and Music.

Dreams come in many different forms, shapes, and sizes. Here are the seven areas of dreams.

1. Health Dreams
2. Financial Dreams
3. Relationship Dreams
4. Self-Development Dreams
5. Adventure Dreams
6. Spirituality/Being Dreams
7. Sharing/Legacy Dreams

Health Dreams. Your body is your vehicle to your dreams. It allows you to move through the world and focus on those people and aspirations that mean the most to you. In a very important way, your health is a wealth multiplier. When you feel vibrant and energized, you are able to accomplish so much more, and enjoy a sense of ease and well-being. What have you dreamed about your health? What weight would you be at? How often would you work out? How strong, flexible, graceful, or fit would you be? The world is your playground, and your physical health gives you greater access to play and explore.

David's Story

It's been a lot of years since I was playing on the United States National Field Hockey Team and training to play in the Olympics. Like any retired athlete, over time my body has changed. When I was in my early twenties, I could do no wrong. I could eat everything I saw, stay up to all hours, and run, and run, and run the next morning. Well, that's not how it works now. When I look at food, I absorb the calories. When I stay up all night, the next morning I'm tired. And when I run, my body lets me know when it's time to stop.

Still, I think in many ways I am healthier now than I was back in the days when I was a professional athlete. I've learned there is a big difference between health and fitness.

(continued)

David's Story *(continued)*

Personally, I've chosen to have both in my life. If you ask me what inspires me to exercise and eat healthfully each day, I'd give you two answers. First is my *big* big health dream—to run, laugh, dance, twirl, spin, and swim with my children, grandchildren, and great-grandchildren. As you can imagine, since I'm only 36 years old, and Heather and I are just starting to have kids, that big dream encompasses a lot of years. But this dream calls to me and moves me.

Second, I create smaller health dreams that make staying healthy and fit fun. The one that I am working on this year is to be able to healthfully complete in one day 500 push ups, 1,000 crunches, and 30 pull-ups. For me, that's a symbolic goal and in order to reach it I need to workout regularly.

Brainstorm Your Health Dreams

For instance, to joyfully maintain a weight of 170 pounds.

For instance, to healthfully complete a short-course triathalon.

_____

_____

_____

_____

Financial Dreams. Money and what you do with it often determines the quality of your life and the lives of others around you. Your financial dreams are often the easiest to quantify. How much passive income do you want? How much wealth do you desire? What are your financial dreams?

Kelly's Story

Kelly and her husband, Rob, were $77,000 in bad debt. They owed $77,000 in revolving debt. Then, three years later, they hit their goal of becoming millionaires.

Kelly and Rob did that by doing exactly the opposite of what most people think you should do. They quit their jobs as LA Police Officers. Just think about that. They had to quit their jobs in order to get rich!

Now, looking back, Kelly shared what that million dollars meant three years ago and what it means today. Three years ago, it felt like an impossible dream. Now, three years later, it just feels like a little step along her path to great wealth.

How did they do it? Again, Kelly tells us that they did it by playing by the rules of the rich. Most people who are doomed to stay middle class don't hire advisors. Or, if they do, they don't take their advice.

Kelly and Rob said that was one of the big things they had to get over. It's not a waste of money to hire advisors. They needed to get advice from people who had done things differently than they had. In fact, Kelly recounts that the single biggest difference between them and other people is that they don't second guess their advisors.

Kelly and Rob had a very clear dream and came up with a plan to get there. They never strayed from that dream and the plan. In fact, it became too easy, they said. The dream provided the focus of what they wanted.

As Emeritus Graduates of Maui Mastermind,* Kelly and Rob embody the spirit of being Maui Millionaires.

Now, it's time for new dreams! We're excited to see what this dynamic young couple comes up with next.

*Emeritus Graduates of Maui Mastermind are participants who have not only attended Maui Mastermind three times, but who have had a positive impact on the Maui community and proven that they are doers who dream big and consistently work to make their dreams, and other people's, come true.

Brainstorm Your Financial Dreams

For instance, to create a passive residual income of $25,000 per month.

For instance, to have a net worth of $2 million within 12 months.

_____

_____

_____

_____

Relationship Dreams. Relationship dreams are the dreams you have of the people in your life and your interactions and relationships with them. What do you dream about your relationships with the people closest to you? These relationships could include ones that currently exist, or they could be about having a new special someone enter your life.

Diane's Story

In 2005, my husband Richard and I adopted a teenage boy from a Mexican orphanage that Maui Mastermind helped support. Once we made the decision to adopt David, it became impossible for us to not be involved in the orphanage he was at. The decision itself changed our lives forever.

Then, once David was with us in our Phoenix home, a short comment by me went on to have even bigger consequences. I explained to him that an adoption meant you got to choose your family, or words to that effect. David quickly went on to adopt aunts and uncles that he wanted in his family. One of his new aunts was Amy at my office. When David met Amy's biological nephew, Caylor, he was puzzled. "I don't understand how she's your aunt. She's my aunt too," Caylor asked.

(continued)

Diane's Story *(continued)*

David calmly explained that his mom (that's me) had told him that when you were adopted you got to pick your family. So, he picked Amy as his aunt, and that meant he picked Caylor as his cousin. Caylor thought for a minute and then decided that it was really great to have an older cousin.

David had a relationship dream of a family, and when he didn't get exactly what he wanted in the beginning, he created it. That's a case of having a dream and seeing it through, and in the process, transforming a whole lot of lives!

Brainstorm Your Relationship Dreams

For instance, to have a lifelong romance and friendship with my spouse.

For instance, to lovingly raise my children to become healthy, happy, independent members of society.

_____

_____

_____

_____

Self-Development Dreams. There is so much to learn in life. What are the areas you want to learn and grow in? Do you want to learn a new language? Or perhaps you want to better understand and love yourself? How about writing a book someday? What are the dreams you have in the area of your own personal development and growth?

Brainstorm Your Self-Development Dreams

For instance, to become fluent in Spanish and a third language.

For instance, to learn to really understand, accept, and love the person I am.

_____

_____

_____

_____

Adventure Dreams. Helen Keller once said that life was either a daring adventure or nothing at all. What are the adventure dreams you have? Do you want to go skydiving? Or hike on the Great Wall of China? Perhaps you want to learn how to white-water kayak, ballroom dance, or drive a Formula One race car? There are so many options available to you in today's world to pursue your adventure dreams that it's a tragic loss to never follow these dreams.

Gathoni's Story

Gathoni attended her first Maui Mastermind event with the goal of becoming a real estate investor. It seemed like a rational decision, but it never really spoke to her passions. Up until then she had been a college professor, so it was a big stretch for her to commit to something so different.

Imagine her surprise when she started really looking at what her Big Dreams were, as part of a special process we do in Maui, and discovered she didn't want to invest in real estate. She truly felt the support of the Maui environment, and, in that freedom, she was able to recognize what she really wanted. Her real dream had always been to become an actress.

(continued)

Gathoni's Story *(continued)*

She went to an audition as soon as she got back from Maui and was cast in a play based on South African stories. The message of the play was as compelling as the fact that she just immediately stepped into her dream life. Some of her fellow Maui Masterminders attended the play, and that also spoke volumes to her about the support that she received from her mastermind group.

Her vision is even clearer now. She is aggressively pursuing a film-making career that will impact lives. She never knew she could have what was really in her heart until she took the time, with a lot of support, to look to what was really there.

Brainstorm Your Adventure Dreams

For instance, go hot air ballooning.

For instance, learn to rock climb and rappel.

_____

_____

_____

_____

Spirituality/Being Dreams. These dreams are about who you are in the world. What is your relationship with your spirituality? This could manifest as your relationship with God through your religion or maybe it's your deep commitment to values and principles that you choose to guide your life. Some people say it's the summation of the eulogy at their funeral. What are your biggest dreams for the man or woman you want to become?

Brainstorm Your Spirituality/Being Dreams

For instance, grow my relationship with God and deepen my faith.

For instance, to live my life consistent with my highest values of peace of mind, love, and joy.

_____

_____

_____

_____

Sharing/Legacy Dreams. One important measure of your life is what you have given. What are your sharing dreams? What are the groups, causes, and organizations that inspire you to support them? What do you want to leave behind as a legacy to future generations? What about the nonfinancial gifts you want to pass on?

David's Story

Diane and I look at both Maui Mastermind and the Maui Millionaires as leveraged vehicles for giving. For us now, when we start a business, we look for a direct way to use that business to positively impact the world. In fact, we have a very big giving dream. We dream that by the year 2020 we will have joyfully and healthfully raised over $200 million for charitable causes and organizations. To be frank, that goal scares us both in a good way. We've raised several million so far, but we have a long way to go without an exact map of how we're going to do it. And that's okay. We'll figure it out along the way. The dream inspires us to write books like this. (In case you haven't caught on yet about how we're doing our best to convince you to make a ton of money and give a lot of it away to charity, just wait until you hit Part Five; that's when we bring out the big guns!)

When I go in to "work" each day, I say to myself, _Today I get to touch people's lives._ It focuses me and inspires me to put in my very best and to savor the gifts I get to share. What causes or dreams inspire you to show up each day in your life?

Brainstorm Your Sharing/Legacy Dreams

For instance, to help every homeless person in my community have safe, compassionate, and dignified ways to get food and shelter and options to help transition back into self sufficiency if they are able and wanting to choose that option.

For instance, to mentor teens so that they can create magnificent lives for themselves.

Three Steps to Make Your Big Dreams Real

Go back through each of the seven areas you brainstormed big dreams on. Select the one Big Dream from each area that moves you the most. Coming up next, you'll work with these seven big dreams to turn them from dreams into a clear, focused, and powerful call to action.

Dreams are most fragile at the moment when they are created. It is at their birth that they most need nurturing. You begin to give your Big Dreams reality and dimension by committing them to paper. You start to build momentum by identifying and committing to one step within the next 72 hours. You generate leveraged power by masterminding with other like-minded people on a clear plan of action to turn your Big Dreams into tangible reality.

The Synergy of Dreams

Synergy is the magic multiplication that comes when two or more elements are combined in such a way that the end result is so much more than just the sum of the parts. We've all experienced synergy in our lives. It occurs when we combine several ideas in such a way that we create a breakthrough or when we work with a special group of people who do something extraordinary that no one thought we could.

This might possibly be the single most powerful force to help you achieve your dreams.

Combine two or more of the dreams into one project. It's more than just killing two birds with one stone. There is a synergy that comes from putting more than one dream on the line. You'll get leverage on yourself to make sure it happens.

For example, let's say you have a dream of a great relationship with your daughter by being the best parent possible, and you want to instill in her a pride in who she is and all that she can be. Now, let's say you also have a financial dream to create passive income through your business so that money will flow through to you easily and automatically. Combine the two, and bring your daughter along with you on the journey. She'll learn that she can have big wealth dreams of her own and she'll never struggle with the feelings of scarcity in her life that so many others have had to overcome. Knowing that is the end result, how can you possibly be too tired or become discouraged with fulfilling your Financial Big Dream? You have a Relationship Big Dream on the line now too.

When you combine dreams, you'll be able to pull other people into them. A person may be excited to participate in one dream and not so interested in another. When you can combine the two, you'll have a wider circle of people interested in making the group project succeed.

Ultimately, the best result with making your Big Dream happen is going to be when you bring other people into the dream. And the only way you're going to tap into the passion that they personally feel is when they are having one of their Big Dreams fulfilled as well. The synergy of dreams means that you include more people in your circle to help make this come true.

Now, let's exercise your synergy muscle.

1 STEP ONE

In the spaces provided below, write down your most moving dream in each of the seven areas. Make sure your Big Dream is clear so that when you share it with other people, they will instantly see what you want to have happen and can support you in your dream.

Health Dream _____
_____

Financial Dream _____
_____

Relationship Dream _____
_____

Self-Development Dream _____
_____

Adventure Dream _____
_____

Spiritual/Being Dream _____
_____

Sharing/Legacy Dream _____
_____

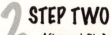

STEP TWO

After each Big Dream, write down one, specific, action step you can take in the next 72 hours to further along this dream. This action step needs to be something that is totally within your control and behaviorally based. This means that if Diane and David were right there by your side they could watch you do this specific action step and know you had completed it.

Health Dream Next Step _____

_____

Financial Dream Next Step _____

_____

Relationship Dream Next Step _____

_____

Self-Development Dream Next Step _____

_____

Adventure Dream Next Step _____

_____

Spiritual/Being Dream Next Step _____

_____

Sharing/Legacy Next Step _____

_____

STEP THREE

Mastermind with at least one other person you respect and trust on how you can make your seven Big Dreams actually happen. What skills will you need to build? What areas will you need to learn about? Who can help you make this dream happen? How can you connect with them? Together, create a working draft of an action plan for each of your seven Big Dreams. Recognize that it doesn't matter if your action plans aren't perfect; what matters is that you get started, and adjust your plan along the way. Feedback is the magic ingredient that helps turn impossible dreams into tangible reality.

Three Potential People to Mastermind with:	Phone Number	Date by which you will have contacted them
_____	_____	_____
_____	_____	_____
_____	_____	_____

Exercise 1: Synergy from Combining Your Big Dreams

Review each of the Big Dreams you have for the major areas. Now brainstorm 10 ways to combine two or more of your Big Dreams in such a way that the result is even better, more exciting, more fulfilling, or more impactful than those items would be individually.

How is it more powerful to combine the dreams?

Exercise 2: Synergy from Combining Your Big Dream with Others' Dreams

This is an exercise that would work really well after you form your Big Dream Mastermind group in Part Three. Together, review your Big Dreams for each of the major categories. Now brainstorm 10 ways to combine one or more of your dreams with one or more of another team member's dreams in such a way that the result is even better.

Exercise 3: Synergy from Your Talents

Share with your team your unique talents. Together with your team, brainstorm 10 ways to create leveraged synergy by combining one or more of your unique talents with one or more of your big dreams in such a way that the result will be a profitable, fun, lucrative, and fulfilling business venture. The goal here is to train your brain so that it can't help but to see money-making opportunities as you live your life. Then use those ideas to tap into the part of you that you enjoy most.

Exercise 4: Synergy from Combining Your Talents with Others

This is another group activity. Pick a start person. This person turns to the person to his right. Have this person share with the group his unique talents. Together as a team, brainstorm 10 ways to create leveraged synergy by combining one or more of his unique talents with one or more of the person to his right's unique talents in such a way that the result will be a profitable, fun, lucrative, and fulfilling business venture. You are starting the lifelong project of learning how to effectively tap into the talents of other people to begin getting the ultimate leverage of other people's time, knowledge, and systems.

The power of synergy works in a number of ways. There is a synergy that comes from combining your own dreams together in an innovative way. Then there is a synergy that occurs when you take one of your dreams and combine it with some else's dream. Finally, there is a synergy that happens when you take someone else's unique talent and use it with your dream. Many people find this single skill—the ability to spot your and others' unique talents—is the most powerful in creating lasting, sustainable businesses that work, so you don't have to!

Create a Mastermind

We'll go into how to create and run a mastermind group in the next part, but for now let's just examine how having a group of like-minded people who bring a different set of talents and experiences together can help you achieve your dreams.

The mastermind group concept was originally discussed in the influential and breakthrough book *Think and Grow Rich* by Napoleon Hill. The idea is that people who work together positively focused on one chief aim will get better and bigger results than just one person working alone. In a mastermind group, everyone gets breakthrough results in a way that just isn't possible working in isolation.

There are three secret powers to tap into within your mastermind group. They are:

1. Power of Reference
2. Power of Network
3. Power of Accountability

Secret 1: The Power of Reference

Many people give up on their Big Dreams simply because they don't believe it's possible to achieve them. They doubt they can do it. Sure, maybe someone else could, but not little, old them. They live in a world that looks for reasons why it can't be done, or why it can't be done by them.

One powerful way to break this pattern and ignite your belief in the possibility that your Big Dream will come true is to become a collector of references. References are the supports and examples that one of your big dreams really is possible. They can come from experiences that you've personally had or from experiences that other people you know about have had. In fact, you can even harvest references from movies, books, or your imagination. References are examples that show one of your Big Dreams is doable.

Are you ready to flex your reference-creation muscle?

Choose a Big Dream from your list that really scares you. If none of them scare you, go back to your brainstormed list of Big Dreams in the seven key areas and supersize one of your dreams. You want to be a little, or a lot, scared of the dream.

Now, brainstorm with your mastermind team all the potential references that show your Big Dream really is doable. These references should spark you with the possibility that you can achieve your Big Dream. Come up with at least 20 references that show that your Big Dream is real, possible, and doable.

Secret 2: The Power of the Network

One of the most important benefits of your mastermind group is that you gain access to the contacts that each member has spent a lifetime cultivating. The average person knows over 100 people. Each of those people knows another 100 more. That means that a mastermind group of eight people directly knows 800 people and indirectly knows everyone on the planet, at least hypothetically. That's the exponential power of the mastermind group.

Now, let's consciously work your network muscle.

Share your list of Big Dreams with your team. Ask each team member to find eight contacts that can help you create, achieve, amplify, or more fully enjoy any of your Big Dreams. Now, it's possible that some of your team members might not be able to find eight contacts for each and every dream. That's okay. In that group of contacts, there will be people who can make a significant difference in you achieving your Big Dream.

There is an additional benefit as well. You and your mastermind team are training your brains so that you begin to be always thinking in terms of *Who do I know who can help this teammate create magic?* Plus, you are starting to think how the rich do—in terms of networks.

Secret 3: The Power of Accountability

If you're accountable, that means you are willing to acknowledge responsibility to others and that you are willing to fully accept responsibility for the actions you take. Period. No excuses.

You've identified your Big Dreams, created a well-rounded field of dreams, and looked for the synergy within the dreams. You've got some additional power working through your mastermind group, regarding networking and reference making.

Now, this is where it comes down to it. Has all this been a mental exercise, or are you prepared to do something to get it done that might feel uncomfortable? In fact, we'll take an even stronger stand and say it *will* feel uncomfortable. If your dream is big enough, it's going to stretch you. You will always feel the stretch.

Are you ready to flex your accountability muscle?

Make a verbal *and* written commitment to your mastermind group to complete one specific step on each of your Big Dreams within the next 72 hours, within the next week, and within the next month. These are three actions you are committing to do on each dream. The commitment is to yourself and to your mastermind group. Make sure each of the actions you are committing to is clear, precise, and fully within your control. In fact, we suggest that your action commitments are behaviorally based, which means that an outside party can see whether you have done them or not.

Then, within your mastermind group, commit to regular meetings to give updates on the progress. The progress report should consist of three parts:

1. What the action item was.

2. The time period in which it was done.

3. What you discovered or accomplished during this time that was important.

For each action item that was scheduled during that time period, list these three items. Give a copy of the Maui Accountability Report to each one of your mastermind group members at the meeting. Then, remember to celebrate the victory!*

This works because you are accountable to someone else. It's a powerful motivator to look good to someone else, and that's what you've set yourself up to do here. You don't want to look bad or let your team down.

You're also creating a written record of what you do. There is a simple yes or no to the question of whether you did it. In fact, don't give yourself enough room on the form to write down the story you'll want to tell if you didn't get it done. "The dog ate my homework" isn't going to fly here.

---

*To download a FREE copy of the Maui Accountability Report simply go to **www.MauiMillionaireBook.com** right now. For full details see the Appendix.

If you don't do what you said you would do, you have a specific, written track record of where the oops occurred, and you have the chance to make corrections along the way.

And, finally, you're locking the action items into your new pattern of how you operate in life. You have employed a number of learning techniques that anchor the action and result in your mind. You are firmly on the side of a doer, as an active participant in the game of life!

In Part Three, we'll share with you more tangible strategies to tap into the awesome power of a mastermind group. But first we want to share with you the five essential ingredients to making your Big Dreams come true.

CHAPTER 10

The Five Essential Ingredients for Making Your Big Dreams Come True

All men dream: but not equally. Those who dream
by night in the dusty recesses of their minds, wake
in the day to find that it was vanity: but the dreamers
of the day are dangerous men, for they may act on
their dreams with open eyes, to make them possible.
—THOMAS EDWARD LAWRENCE (of Arabia)

The beginning of a dream is when it's most fragile. Chances are you've been here before. You've seen a dream die before. And that has meant that you've built up references on what it means to have a dream and more importantly, how easy it is to lose a dream.

The dying of a dream is the single most devastating thing that can happen to a thinking, caring human being. Think about it—every time something hasn't worked out for you, a dream has died. Every tragedy is a tragedy because it was a dream that is gone. An investment that lost you money is a financial dream that collapsed. A natural devastation that wipes out part of a family is the death of a relationship dream. These may be old pains associated with losing a dream that are so deep that they choke off hope of ever having a dream again.

Yet we're telling you that you need to dream again. And, not only that, we want you to supersize your dreams. And we want you to create a whole field of dreams that inspire you each day of your life.

David's Story

I lived 10 years of my life with the single-minded focus of playing in the Olympics. It was the dream and goal that defined that era of my life. And I failed.

Oh, I'm not talking about the fact that I got injured and wasn't able to compete in the Olympics—that wasn't my real failure. The real failure was how for the last six years of my dream I kept pushing back the day I would celebrate and enjoy my journey to the precise moment when I attained it. I even asked my dad to not come watch me compete until he could see me in the Olympics so that he would see me at my pinnacle moment.

I smile as I share this because I recognize and am so grateful for the lessons this experience taught me. In fact, I wouldn't trade the lessons and experience back in to get success in this dream. What I really learned was that it is a costly mistake to live your life focused on the day your dream comes true. The real juice and joy in life come when you are actively engaged in your life, dreaming big and playing full out, and enjoying every step along the way. Why only enjoy and celebrate for the one transitory moment at the top? Instead, savor the journey and drink deeply from the experiences along the way.

I look back, and what do I miss most about my hockey days? Two things. I miss playing hockey every day—the training sessions. And I miss how good it felt to be in that kind of elite-level physical condition. Funny how these were two of the things I most took for granted and even ignored while I was experiencing them. After all, I had a dream to pursue and no time to waste on the joy of the journey. Sometimes, life's best lessons come wrapped in irony. God's got to be smiling.

I share this story with you because I want you to remember that as you dream big dreams and go after them with all you've got, savor the journey. In the end it guarantees you'll be successful, no matter what the outcome.

If you've come this far: Congratulations! It's taken a lot to think about what you really want in your life. That's especially true if you haven't always gotten what you wanted.

Now let's look at the five key ingredients that will assure your success in making your Big Dreams come true in a way that is meaningful and joyous.

Ingredient One: Humility

One of the five essential ingredients that will help you achieve and enjoy your Big Dreams is the quality of humility. This is not something we commonly talk about in our culture, nor is it a quality most people consciously develop.

A person with humility will make the effort to listen to and accept others. In today's world, we often think it takes being loud, brash, and arrogant to be heard. But the secret of humility tells us that the person who accepts others is held in higher esteem. One word spoken in humility is heard before a thousand clashing words.

Humility is based on self-respect. With self-respect, there is knowledge of one's own strength and the acceptance and appreciation of others. Humility allows you to grow with dignity and integrity. With humility, arrogance disappears. Humility allows lightness in the face of challenges.

When a person seeks to impress, dominate, or limit the freedom of others in order to prove his own self worth, the exact opposite occurs. The dominating person actually diminishes his own inner feelings of worth, dignity, and peace of mind.

Are you ready to exercise your humility muscle? These exercises and the ones that follow require a partner. This needs to be someone you trust, perhaps someone in your mastermind group.

Exercise 1

Take 60 seconds and jot down a "failure" that you have experienced in your life. Now, next to that failure, write down the lesson it taught you. Maybe it taught you to savor the journey, or that people matter more than possessions, or that you are stronger than you knew. What did you learn from that failure?

_____

_____

Openly share your failure and what you learned from it. Ask your partner to do the same.

Pay attention to your inner experience as this happens. Are you really listening to your partner's experience, or are you obsessing over the failure you shared? Are you surprised by what your partner shared as to what her failure meant? Can you relate?

Now, the big question. How do you feel about your partner? Do you feel more connected and bonded? Do you accept your partner more or less now that she has been completely open with you to share a time when something didn't work for her?

What's the lesson that you can learn from this about the need to be perfect to be accepted?

Now would be a great time to tell your partner about what you experienced when she shared her failure.

The more full out you're willing to do this experience, the bigger the results you'll get.

The only people who make mistakes are the people who are actually doing something. If you are a doer, as we define a Maui Millionaire, you're going to make mistakes. Humility helps us see these mistakes with a sense of lightness as learning experiences.

Exercise 2

A big part of humility is to cultivate the fine art of laughter, especially the kind of laughter that you enjoy when you see how seriously you are taking yourself.

Take 60 seconds, and jot down a moment when you had a good laugh at how seriously you were taking yourself. Ask your partner to do the same. What happened, and how did you feel after you started to laugh at yourself? How did your laughter influence you and the situation?

_____

_____

Share your experiences with your partner.

Exercise 3

Sometimes, we let our pride or the feeling of spite stop us from benefiting from the lessons we could learn from people or situations we don't like or enjoy.

Take 60 seconds, and jot down a time when you learned something (or could have learned something) from a person you didn't like. What was the lesson (or what could have been the lesson)? Learning this lesson from that person in that situation impacted your life in what way?

_____

_____

Discuss your answers with your partner and listen as he discusses his. What insights did you have as a result of learning about his failure?

Exercise 4

Together with your partner, brainstorm ten ways you can cultivate the quality of humility in your own life.

1. _____
2. _____
3. _____
4. _____
5. _____
6. _____
7. _____
8. _____
9. _____
10. _____

Ingredient Two: Faith

Frequently, we think of faith in only a religious sense. And that is obviously an important aspect, but faith is much more. Faith is a living, creative, active, and powerful thing. Faith doesn't stop to ask if good works ought to be done, but has already done them and continues to do them without ceasing.

Still faith is more than that.

Faith is the basis of business. Over 95 percent of the commerce of the world is on credit. It's faith that makes us trust that the paper currency we receive is actually worth something more than just the paper. If the public loses faith in the stability of the money market, immediate and complete financial panic ensues. Every industry rests upon faith. Every financial enterprise has only faith for its foundation.

Faith is the basis of society. Without faith in each other, families fall apart. Break down confidence in a government, and revolution soon follows. Without faith in something, you cannot accomplish anything worthwhile.

The central quality that will help you achieve and enjoy your Big Dreams is the quality of faith. Philosophers have argued about faith for thousands of years, but you and I each have a clear feeling of what faith means to us. And, that's what matters most. The challenge is that in our hectic lives sometimes we allow faith—in ourselves, in our dreams, in humanity, in God—to be crowded out. Most people do not consciously develop their faith muscles, but then, you are not most people. Here's your chance to get a little faith workout.

Exercise 1

Take 60 seconds, and jot down what faith means to you. This is a deeply personal thing. What is it for you?

_____

_____

Briefly share what faith is for you with a partner. As you listen to your partner's response, notice the common elements between your answers. Notice how your partner adds unique flavors and textures to her understanding of what faith means. The sameness and the differences are exactly as they should be.

Exercise 2

Why do you believe that the world is a miraculous place?

Together with your partner, brainstorm 10 miracles you see in everyday life.

1. _____

2. _____

3. _____

4. _____

5. _____

6. _____

7. _____

8. _____

9. _____

10. _____

Exercise 3

Together with your partner, brainstorm 10 ways you can cultivate the quality of faith in your own life.

1. _____

2. _____

3. _____

4. _____

5. _____

6. _____

7. _____

8. _____

9. _____

10. _____

Ingredient Three: Integrity

Integrity is a value, like humility and faith. Even more than that, it is the value that guarantees all the other values. You are a person of integrity to the degree to which you live your life consistent with your highest values. Integrity is the quality that locks in your values and inspires you to live consistently with them.

What does it take to have integrity? Integrity is the foundation of character. It requires that you be impeccably honest with yourself. You must be true to the very best that is in you and to the very best that you know. When you commit to living this kind of life, you will find yourself continually raising your own standards. Integrity is taking responsibility when you don't live up to your word, as all of us will from time to time, being the imperfect human beings we are. In these moments, you live integrity by refusing to make up excuses and instead owning your choices and behavior. From this place, you can make new choices, including the choice to do things differently next time. It's a place of authentic power and real freedom.

Perhaps the most important test of your level of integrity will be the measurement of your life. Your life only becomes better when you become better. Life is lived from the inside out. Your values determine the kind of person you really are. They are what you stand for, and what you won't stand for. Your level of integrity tells you and the world the kind of person you have become.

Integrity is the quality most demanded of leaders. It is expressed in terms of constancy and consistency. It is manifested in an absolute devotion to keeping one's word. Integrity builds the confidence that others have in you.

> **If honesty did not exist, it would have to be invented**
> **as it is the surest way of getting rich.**
> **—EARL NIGHTINGALE**

There are three primary areas of your life where acting with integrity becomes most evident.

The first area of integrity has to do with your relationships with your family and your friends. Being true to yourself means living in truth with each person in your life. It means refusing to say or do something that you don't believe is right.

The second area of integrity has to do with your attitude and behavior toward money. Casualness toward money brings casualties in your financial life. Be fastidious about your treatment of money, and guard your credit rating the same way you would guard your honor.

The third area of integrity has to do with your commitments to others, especially in your business, your work, and your investment activities. Always keep your word. If you say that you will do something, do it. If you make a promise, keep it. If you make a commitment, fulfill it. Be known as the kind of person that can always be trusted, no matter what the circumstances. And when those times come where you find you haven't lived up to your word, take responsibility and make amends as best you can. Renegotiate your commitments, if need be.

Integrity is a choice, and by choosing to live your life to this higher standard your Big Dreams become possible. Integrity also recognizes that the way in which you pursue your Big Dreams is every bit as important as attaining them. The problem is that most people do not consciously develop their integrity muscles.

Exercise 1

Take 60 seconds, and jot down a time when you didn't live up to a commitment. Why didn't you honor your commitment? Notice that your habitual first answer may be to look outside of yourself for a cause for not fulfilling your commitment. If this is the case, go deeper and jot down how you could have taken responsibility.

_____

_____

   Discuss this with your partner. As you briefly share the experience, notice how it feels to share this. Is it freeing to admit you weren't perfect? Is it scary to share this? Perhaps you, like us, will find it to be both these things.

Exercise 2

Take 60 seconds, and jot down a time when you made a hard decision not to do something because you knew in your heart it simply wasn't right. It may have been easy, or convenient, or profitable, but you just knew it wasn't the right thing to do. How did you feel as you made this decision? Did you struggle? Was it easy?

_____

_____

   Discuss this with your partner. Listen with your eyes, ears, and heart to your partner. What did each of you have in common? How do you feel about your partner after listening to the integrity she has?

Exercise 3

Together, brainstorm 10 ways you can cultivate the quality of integrity in your own life.

1. _____

2. _____

3. _____

4. _____

5. _____

6. _____

7. _____

8. _____

9. _____

10. _____

Ingredient Four: Courage

It takes a lot of courage to stand up for what's right when we have to take a risk to do so. But many people are under the mistaken impression that courage means you are fearless. After all, we are flooded with media images of larger than life heros and heroines who face all kinds of crises without a moment's hesitation or fear.

But courage is only possible for someone who feels fear and takes action in the presence of that fear. Courage is a quality of greatness and an essential part of achieving Big Dreams. It's the enforcing virtue, the one that makes possible all the other virtues common to exceptional leaders: honesty, integrity, confidence, compassion, and humility. In short, leaders who lack courage cannot be effective leaders.

We're all afraid of something. The one fear we must all guard against is the fear of ourselves. You have a courage muscle. The more you exercise it, the stronger it gets. The problem is that most people do not consciously develop their courage muscles by consistently finding ways to stretch their comfort zone. Maui Millionaires have all found ways to stretch themselves by taking calculated risks. They have pushed themselves to ask for things in negotiations that were scary for them to ask for. And they've faced commitments they couldn't incrementally inch across, but instead had to leap with all their might, fully committing to move and committed to their decision. Here's your chance to work out your courage muscles!

Exercise 1

Take 60 seconds, and jot down a time when you were afraid. What was going on in your environment at that moment? What was the story you made up about what that all meant?

_____

_____

Now share this experience with your partner. Do your best to separate out the objective facts from the meanings you have given to those facts.

Notice how much easier it is to distinguish the fact from the story when it's the other person who is sharing versus when it is you who is sharing. One of the most important parts of cultivating courage is to become aware of all the ways we heighten our own fear by making up scary interpretations to the events of our lives. Take a few minutes, and discuss your insights with your partner.

Exercise 2

One of the areas we need all our courage is in the area of love. We all have a fundamental need for love, and we all fear its withdrawal.

Take 60 seconds, and jot down a time when you made yourself vulnerable to love. What was the scariest part to you about opening up and being vulnerable at that moment? What was the outcome? As you briefly share the experience with your partner, savor the flavor of the memory— whether it be pure joy or bittersweet.

_____

_____

Exercise 3

Together, brainstorm 10 ways you can cultivate the quality of courage in your own life.

1. _____

2. _____

3. _____

4. _____

5. _____

6. _____

7. _____

8. _____

9. _____

10. _____

Ingredient Five: Gratitude

Gratitude is the full appreciation of something in your life. It's the ultimate expression of joy in that moment of full realization of your life, existence, and belonging. In a moment of gratitude, you do not discriminate. Instead you pay careful attention and notice. It's your awareness that gives life to your appreciation as you really see and accept things as they are and for all that they contain. It's the fastest shortcut to becoming aware of how wealthy you already are.

When gratitude is this well established, it is a sign of a heart that has been made right and whole. Gratitude can't coexist with arrogance, resentment, or selfishness.

> **Gratitude rejoices with her sister joy and is always ready to light a candle and have a party. Gratitude doesn't much like the old cronies of boredom, despair, and taking life for granted.**
> **—REBBE NACHMAN of Breslov**

Are you ready to stretch your gratitude muscles?

Exercise 1

Take 60 seconds, and jot down three things you are grateful for right now in your life. Why are you grateful for that person, situation, or thing? What can you do to show your appreciation more?

_____

_____

Discuss the three items of gratitude with your partner. As you listen to your partner discuss his items of gratitude, feel the warmth that comes when a person is a state of gratitude. Does he feel more present and aware at that time? More peaceful? Take a minute and just enjoy that feeling.

Exercise 2

Take 60 seconds and jot down a time when a relationship ended or an experience expired that you hadn't previously expressed gratitude for. What about that lost relationship or situation made you grateful, even though you didn't show your gratitude at the time?

_____

_____

Discuss the circumstances with your partner and now, belatedly, express your gratitude for what you had. If it's appropriate, get in contact with those other people and share with them how you feel.

Exercise 3

Brainstorm together 10 ways that you can experience more gratitude in your life on a regular basis.

1. _____

2. _____

3. _____

4. _____

5. _____

6. _____

7. _____

8. _____

9. _____

10. _____

Faith, humility, integrity, courage, and gratitude—these are the traits of Maui Millionaires. Become a leader in your own life by setting a course to make your Big Dreams come true. The biggest danger we face is losing our ability to dream. Keep yours alive. Don't just cultivate the ability to dream, but learn to stretch and expand your dreams so that they inspire, move, and empower you to live a life of greatness and joy.

CHAPTER 11

Playing the Maui Millionaire Big Dream Game

In the past two chapters, we went through the components for creating and then implementing your Big Dreams. This is often an uncomfortable area for people the first time they go through it. That's simply because most of us have forgotten how to dream.

We want to help you reconnect with your Big Dreams and the belief that they can all come true for you. The past few chapters had exercises to get you going. Now, we'd like to invite you to combine your Big Dream with the power of synergy and supersize it.

We've created a fun, engaging game for you and your closest friends or mastermind partners to play to explore your Big Dreams and create tangible breakthroughs to make them real. We call it the Maui Millionaire Big Dream Game™, and we would like to give you the game as our free gift. It's a small way that we can support you in living the life you want and becoming a Maui Millionaire.

To get your free copy of this game simply go to **www.MauiMillionaire Book.com** and click on the "Big Dream" tab. Once there, you will be able to download the game and start playing right away. We have purposefully kept the game simple because fancy bells and whistles won't generate real results for you. The real power will come when you use the Maui Millionaire

Big Dream Game as a spring board to supersize your dreams and support others as they work to realize their dreams.

Two Secrets of Playing the Maui Millionaire Big Dream Game

There are two main reasons why the Maui Millionaire Big Dream Game will help you bring back your Big Dreams into your life. These two secrets are related to both the foundational emotions that come about when we play games and the synergistic supersizing that occurs when we act on something together with like-minded people. Put those two secrets together, and the possibilities go through the roof.

The two secrets are these: One, when you lose yourself inside the fun of this game, you will be automatically upgrading your W.O.S.—without struggle or effort. Two, the more emotion you bring to the game, the more powerful the shift in your W.O.S.

Why We Play Games

Nicole Lazzaro wrote a brilliant paper on games and the people who play them entitled, "Why We Play Games: Four Keys to More Emotion Without Story." We've borrowed from her work in reaching the key emotions that will come up for you when you play the Maui Millionaire Big Dream Game. After studying players of a wide variety of games, she identified the four keys to bringing emotion into a game. Once the emotion is engaged, the passion follows, and that's when breakthrough results happen! One word of caution before you go to **www.MauiMillionaireBook.com** to get going on the Maui Millionaire Big Dream Game. You may decide to play the game just to "test it out," but if you play full out, you will be changed. That's because the game engages the emotions to make it real in your life. You will have been stretched beyond where you are now. And, once stretched, you will never go back to your old dimensions.

Hard Fun—Emotions from Meaningful Challenges, Strategies, and Puzzles

These emotions come up from meaningful challenges, strategies, and puzzles. The challenge of hard fun creates frustration, followed by personal triumph. It inspires creativity. The Maui Millionaire Big Dream Game is not a difficult game on the surface. But the more you commit to the game, the harder it becomes. It matches people from different skill levels and allows them to play together because the true playing field isn't really on a game board. It's life that provides the backdrop. There are emotional opportunities that come about because of cooperative game play.

Easy Fun—Grab Attention with Ambiguity, Incompleteness, and Detail

An Easy Fun player gets joy from the process of the game itself. There is a focus on the experience, rather than the need to win. In this state, you feel curiosity, wonder, awe, and mystery as deeper meaning for your own Big Dreams comes about. The best part is exploring new worlds with intriguing people. You get the opportunity to figure something out about yourself.

Altered States—Generate Emotion with Perception, Thought, Behavior, and Other People

The internal experience of a game allows you to enjoy changes in your emotional state during and after play. The game is played outside the body, with other people, but the changes are very personal and vary depending on the player. The player's experience is changed as perception, behavior, and thought combine in a socially-important group to produce emotions. An altered states reaction means that you think or feel something different when it's done. You might feel that you've gone to another level and feel better about yourself and your future.

The People Factor—Create Opportunities for Player Competition, Cooperation, Performance, and Spectacle

An important point from the study is that people will play games they don't like, just so they can spend time with people they do like. The game actually forms and cements friendships. It's a mechanism for social interaction. This is true regardless of whether the game is competitive or cooperative. A mastermind group, by definition, is a cooperative group, so that members are not competing for the best idea or trying to win by having someone else lose. The idea is that when your mastermind group plays the game, it pushes each of you to make new breakthroughs at the same time as you deepen your friendships and relationships.

The four keys to unlock emotions in games are:

1. Hard Fun
2. Easy Fun
3. Altered States
4. The People Factor

The more you can become emotionally committed to your Big Dreams, the more certain their creation. Games allow us to try out new ideas and new ways of being in the world. You get to stretch your muscles in a safe environment. In fact, after just a few times playing the Maui Millionaire Big Dream Game you might just find that your perspective on everything has changed and that you have more wealth flowing to you than you ever thought possible.

Why We Mastermind

A mastermind group is a collection of like-minded people who come together for a specific purpose, and somehow during the process magic occurs. There's a lot more on creating and developing mastermind groups in the coming chapters, but for now, let's consider why a mastermind group is so powerful for playing this game.

The game becomes a reason to get together. It provides a context for the meeting, a focus for a desired result. There is a feeling that we're all in this together as you go through the sometimes challenging or scary process of stretching to create big dreams.

A mastermind group will hold you accountable to the steps you put in place to make your dream come true. You're going to commit to some steps right away and to more steps down the road. We will often feel more pressure to not let our friends down than we will to the commitment we make to ourselves. That's the power of your mastermind group. By holding you accountable they help you be your best self.

In the next few chapters, you'll learn practical advice for running your mastermind meetings. But before you get started, take a moment and go to **www.MauiMillionaireBook.com** and download your free copy of the Maui Millionaire Big Dream Game.

PART THREE

MAUI WEALTH LEVERAGE STRATEGY THREE: Mastermind Your Way to Millions!

CHAPTER 12

You are One Mastermind Group Away from Having Everything You Ever Wanted

> No man is smart enough to project his influences very far into the world without the friendly cooperation of other men. Drive this thought home in every way you can for it is sufficient unto itself to open the door to success in the higher brackets of individual achievement.
> —ANDREW CARNEGIE (World's Wealthiest Person in Early Part of the Twentieth Century)

Ιf you are looking for the real edge that allows some people to outearn others by a factor of 1,000 to one then this section is for you. Now, imagine you get that edge while being able to have a lot more fun working together with people you care about in friendly cooperation. Notice we said "cooperation" not "competition." That's a fundamental part of being a Maui Millionaire. The relationship is as important as the result. You cannot separate the way you go about becoming wealthy from your results.

You'll find that succeeding becomes easy and natural when you tap into this powerful success principal. In fact, it will become like breathing air, something you do automatically, without effort.

You'll find that your life will *feel* more satisfying. Your relationships with other people will get both more particular and more rewarding.

You'll find that you will literally have become a money magnet, attracting into your life the people and circumstances to build great wealth and you'll find that you'll put all that wealth to healthy purposes benefiting others, many of whom you'll never meet or even know about.

So, what is the secret ingredient that will allow you to unlock the door to all this greatness? It's called a Mastermind Group, and it is one of the most powerful tools to building a wealthy and successful life ever discovered.

> **Mastermind [Group]: An alliance of two or more minds blended in a spirit of perfect harmony and cooperating for the attainment of a definite purpose.**
> —NAPOLEON HILL, Author of *Think and Grow Rich*

Napoleon Hill, author of one of the most important self-help best-sellers of all time, once said that the two things every successful man and woman have in common are a burning desire to attain their definite chief goal, and a mastermind alliance that helps them accomplish this goal.

In today's world, we already know the power of a person's peer group influences him in a thousand different ways. You have undoubtedly experienced this subtle but powerful influence in your own life.

What Your Mastermind Group Can Do for You

- Hold you accountable.
- Share contacts.
- Share expertise.
- Share fresh perspective.
- Ask a great question.
- Help you see things through a new model/metaphor/frame of reference.
- Share resources.
- Encourage and support you.

Have you ever hung around a group of negative, stressed out, unhappy, whiney people? How did you feel when you spent time with them? Did you observe that the more they griped and complained, the more you felt negative, critical, and just plain exhausted?

Now think back to when you might have experienced the exact opposite. Have you ever spent time with quality individuals who looked at life through the eyes of eagerness, joy, and faith? How did you feel and act when you were with these people?

If you're like thousands of people we've worked with over the years, you have had tangible experiences of how your peer group's attitude and belief systems rubbed off on you. Just imagine, you can literally install any belief system you choose that supports you in growing and succeeding in life simply by carefully cultivating a peer group of other people who exemplify these beliefs!

We saw earlier how important the Wealth Operating System was in determining your ability to have wealth in your life. Change your W.O.S., and you change everything. Your mastermind group holds the secret to upgrading your Wealth Operating System quickly, easily, and automatically.

But there is one catch, and it's a doozy. Not only do you have to convince these other successful people to want to hang around with you, but you have to cultivate a positive, inspiring environment in which to mastermind in order to have full access to the real power lying in your mastermind group.

Forming Your Mastermind Group

Magic happens when you form a mastermind group to help you take action. You get support, feedback, ideas, and accountability. You've already seen, undoubtedly, in your own life as well as throughout this book, how important it is to carefully choose the people you hang out with and with whom you share your innermost dreams.

And, when it comes to your mastermind group, you've got one more thing you have to protect—the mastermind group itself. A group of people meeting together can be either a committee or a mastermind group. A mastermind group is a group of people who come together for achieving a specific goal. They maintain respect for each other and harmony in the group. They also respect the confidentiality of the group, so that members have a safe place to stretch. A group of people formed as a mastermind group can accomplish more than they ever could individually. A committee is something entirely different.

A committee is a body of individuals who have formed to feel good about themselves or their role in a cause. It could also be a group that has been formed to obscure responsibility. A mastermind group is a special thing in the world. Its purpose is bigger, and the people in it leave the group feeling bigger. Please note. Just because a group is labeled as "committee" or a "mastermind group" doesn't mean that it is one or the other. Some committees become mastermind groups, and some mastermind groups degenerate into committees. It's what the group does that counts.

In a mastermind group, people meld their collective energies, experiences, contacts, and creativity into something more than the sum of the parts. A mastermind group holds you accountable. We join a mastermind group because we know that we are strongly influenced by our peer group, and we know that the way our peer group sees us is often the person we become. Their perceptions of us shape our behavior. When you consciously choose your peer group, you're choosing who you want to be. In life, we were born into our families. It's as we grow and choose our mastermind partners that we start to consciously direct our growth and success.

A mastermind group empowers us to become more than we are now. As our fellow mastermind group partners see us as our best selves, we work like crazy to live up to those qualities, so we won't let them down. We know that they accept us for all that we are, it's just that we find their company inspirational, and it sparks us to work hard to live consistent with that which is best within us.

A mastermind group allows you to share contacts and expertise. We know that one contact might open up a whole new world of possibilities. We add in our special talents with others' special talents so that we grow faster than we could by ourselves. For example, you might have a partner who is great at quantitative analysis, and you're great at negotiation. You can work together to do something even better and learn from each other along the way.

A mastermind group gives you new ideas and fresh energy. There is a collective energy that comes about when we spend time with people who encourage us and cheer us on. As you become more successful, it's even more important that you be conscious about the people with whom you share your successes. Some people will become envious or interpret what your success means to them, rather than simply feeling good about your success. Your mastermind group members will be happy for your success. In fact, the right mastermind group partners will often care more about your success than you do.

There are five keys to get your Mastermind group off to the right start.

1. *Create a single, definite focus for your group.* For example, you might want to have a mastermind group for creating business and financial success, one for accountability, and another for charitable

purpose. It becomes very difficult to try to wrap them all up into one mastermind group, unless you can find a definition that is very broad for the group that encompasses all of the goals. It's the definite shared purpose that draws your mastermind group together and focuses your energy towards one common end.

2. *Ensure that everyone benefits.* If one or two people are doing all the work and not getting a proportionate amount back, it will feel unfair. Pretty soon, at one level or another, they'll simply give up. Not everyone has to benefit in the same way. Benefit is in the eye of the person getting the benefit. Regularly check in and ask your partners, "How are we doing here? Is everyone benefiting?"

3. *Foster respect within the group.* Without respect, it's impossible to fully hear each other because as human beings we cannot fully separate what we hear from how we feel about the person who is delivering the message. It's critical for your group to work hard to always treat each other respectfully, especially when differences are being discussed and emotions may be running high. You must maintain your behaviors so that you treat each other with courtesy and respect.

4. *Maintain harmony.* If your group starts to turn into a gripe session, you have a committee. The moment you change from having a cooperative state and start complaining, it's no longer a mastermind group, rather it's an ordinary committee.

   Treasure the positive polarity of your group. You must all make a committed, conscious decision that you will work from a positive frame and that you will view everything from the highest and best use. If something bad happens to you that you want to discuss with your mastermind group partners, ask them to help you find ways to look at this as a blessing, gift, or lesson.

   While you can question the usefulness of a specific idea for you, never question the intention of the person giving it. If you question the intention, you'll destroy the relationship.

5. *Build trust.* Be impeccable with your word. That means if something didn't go right and a member didn't live up to a commitment, the conversation isn't about the excuses for why it didn't work. Rather, the conversation is about the choices she made. If you have a partner who consistently doesn't do what she said she would do, you need to make a decision regarding that partner. Cherish your mastermind group and protect it so that trust is a benchmark tradition.

Two more things regarding trust in your mastermind group. First, be on time. That's an element of having and running a respectful mastermind group and it means that you'll be impeccable with your word. Second, maintain confidentiality. If you can't stay true to, "What's said in the mastermind group, stays in the mastermind group," it'll be hard to feel open in the mastermind group.

Remember, the entire intent of the mastermind group is to come together to create magic.

Five Laws of a Successful Mastermind Group

1. *Be selective.* Character is contagious. Be careful whose character you catch!

2. *Each member benefits.* No one will give full-hearted cooperation over time without getting some tangible benefit in return. Make sure you work to benefit each member of your mastermind group on a consistent basis.

3. *Maintain harmony.* A mastermind group with tension or conflict is degraded to a simple committee. The single most important rule to maintaining harmony in the group is that while you can question ideas and input, never question intent. If you do, you will destroy the relationship.

4. *Compelling and definite chief aim.* Collectively create a compelling outcome for the group which all of you are fully committed to. This direction will focus your collective power and allow you to harness it to awesome effect.

5. *Maintain confidentiality.* People will be much more open and cooperative if they feel they can let their guard down and authentically and safely share.

We'll cover some techniques for actually running the mastermind group in the rest of this part.

Now, though, let's consider how you're going to find people to invite into your mastermind group. Where can you find the like-minded partners with whom you are willing to entrust your future?

- *Your current peers.* For example, when you're starting out in business or investing, mastermind with other beginning business builders or investors to support and aid each other. If you're a successful entrepreneur, choose other entrepreneurs who have really accomplished things in their business lives. The key for this type of group is to choose people with the right *attitudes*. They need to be people whose *character* you want to catch.

- *Your mentors.* Every investor or business person needs to find a mentor to mastermind with. This is one of the fastest ways to take yourself two or three levels higher in a single step.

- *Your imaginary mentors.* Who are the people you admire from the present day, history, or fiction? Create an imaginary place where you sit and talk with these powerful role models. What qualities do you want to impress into your mind by "meeting" with this group?

My imaginary mastermind group has five members: Gandhi, Leo Buscaglia, Harry Truman, Yoda, and Tony Robbins. A strange blend I know. But Gandhi teaches me the power of faith and congruent living; Leo the power of love; Mr. Truman (I never could call him Harry) teaches me how to live my values and be true to my word; Yoda inspires me to be powerful and humble; and Tony helps me to embrace my greatness.

—DAVID FINKEL

The mastermind group is a significant element in the success and happiness of a Maui Millionaire.

Roger's Story

Roger, a Maui Millionaire who recently moved to Austin, Texas, shared how he did a one-time investment deal in partnership with a fellow Maui Millionaire, Rob. They found that they enjoyed doing that one project together so much that they looked for how they could do more projects together. Not only did they form an investment company together called Grasslands Investments, but they also recruited several other Maui Masterminders to join their company and team.

According to Roger, not only has this mastermind team that focuses on putting together commercial real estate deals made them all money, but it's turned into one of the most rewarding relationships in their lives. They love working with each other and count the friendship and fun they have as they make money one of the biggest benefits of this focused mastermind team.

Together, they've purchased apartment complexes, mobile home parks, and a 342,000-square-foot manufacturing campus. That is the power of your mastermind group.

CHAPTER 13

Six Keys To Minimize Conflict and Maximize Results in Any Mastermind Group

Your mastermind group is a powerful tool to leverage the talents and connections of other people. The biggest danger to a mastermind group is that it may degenerate to a committee. A committee makes people smaller in comparison to whatever agenda item is before the committee. A mastermind group takes an issue and elevates the person so that she is big enough to accept the possibilities in her life and in making her Big Dreams comes true.

Remember the goal is to put a group of people together in such a manner that when they get together magic happens. That only happens when there is trust, respect, focus, harmony, and an atmosphere where everyone benefits.

Arguments within a Mastermind Group

One of the quickest ways to destroy harmony in a group is with an argument. Whenever two or more people have different ideas or opinions, you run the risk of having an argument.

An argument occurs when ideas are viewed as being right or wrong. If one is right, then the other is wrong. And, boy, we hate to be wrong. That leads to defensiveness. You may end up getting to the technical truth, but not the full truth. You'll look for evidence and spins that support your argument. You close down ideas.

When you argue, you get locked into an entrenched position. You can't back down, and before you know it, the idea has morphed into something completely different.

You've lost your mastermind group and now have a committee. But, wait! There is another way.

Parallel Thinking

Another method to handle differing opinions is with something called *parallel thinking*. It's not about asking questions like "Is this correct? Do I agree or disagree?" Instead the goal is to ask: "Where does this idea take us?"

This isn't argument and debate. When two people think different things, put them both on the map. So often, we fall victim to the false trap of deciding something well before we have to. Don't make a decision between the various ideas until a later stage in your discussions. When you are masterminding ideas, the real purpose is just to get the ideas out there and see what the next spark of creativity is. Ideas become stepping stones to new ideas, and before you know it you have created a breakthrough new idea that you never would have reached or created had you been locked into the old-school model of argument and debate.

The old school model of correct/incorrect and agree/disagree leads us into the Big Three:

1. Argument

2. Defensiveness

3. Entrenched Positions

And, that destroys the Mastermind process.

Parallel thinking leads us to a new model of ideas and interactions as movement. There is no right or wrong answer, just put forth another thought, and see where the direction goes. This movement lays out an accurate map. Follow the map, and you can ease your way with small steps that lead to greater things.

One simple way to do this is to append onto someone's comment. Instead of "but," say "and." Then look for where a synergy between those two ideas can take you. That's how brand new ideas are created and breakout thinking occurs.

Make a commitment together in your mastermind group to work toward bigger dreams by avoiding argument and instead engaging in parallel thinking. One of the greatest tools available for mastermind groups are the six Maui Hats™.*

The Six Maui Hats

At a glance, there are six hats that correspond to specific ways of thinking or being. These are:

White Hat: Your professor or thinker mode

Red Hat: Your emotional/intuitive hat

Black Hat: Your bodyguard

Yellow Hat: Your enthused champion

Green Hat: Your creative genius

Blue Hat: Your organizing hat

We'll look at these six hats in more detail in just a minute. But, first, let's look at the benefits of the Maui Hats.

- They let people play and relax into the fun. It's a little like playing dress up. You get to try on a different hat (even if it's just imaginary) and then act a certain way that maybe you're not used to. It's a way to safely try on a new role.

- They reduce people's perceived risk in contributing to the group and help people feel safer playing a role that they put on . . . it's not "them," only a hat they are wearing. People open up when the Six Hats come out.

- They help people avoid argument. As we discussed before, argument is almost always detrimental and destructive. Now you can

---

*The six thinking hats concept was created by Edward de Bono, who pioneered many of the ideas in this chapter. We've included several of his fine books as part of the "Suggested Reading List" we've put up at **www.MauiMillionaireBook.com.** We can't say enough good things about the quality of his ideas.

simply note all sides in parallel and move forward in your master-minding. If in the rare case you need to choose, you lay out the map and eventually let your red hat (emotion) choose.

- They simplify the thinking process. Rather than use all thinking styles all at once in a great big muddle, you can break out the parts and really flesh out the ideas.

- They help people *switch* thinking patterns and avoid thinking ruts. You get to experience different ways of thinking about a challenge or goal in a unique way.

Now, let's look at the six Maui Hats again in greater detail. We'll then go through a couple of exercises that you can do together with your master-mind group to get you going on how to effectively run a mastermind group.

White Hat: The Professor or Thinker Mode

Focus: Exclusively on the objective facts, information and data *without* any interpretation or story. This is your objective thinker mode that lays out known factual information and looks at challenges with the dispassionate, neutral voice of reason.

Questions

What information do we have?

What information do we need?

What information are we missing?

How can we find that information?

What questions would be useful to ask?

What are the facts as we know them?

Key Descriptive Phrases

- Rigorous thinking
- Laying out the known facts
- Mapping out the physical landmarks
- Asking the right questions

Believed Facts versus Confirmed Facts

Before we act on any believed fact that could be crucial to the outcome, make sure to confirm that fact. The White Hat is all about the confirmed facts. Think about a computer processing data. You need to put your White Hat on to give the computer the facts it needs.

Model White Hatters

- Data (from *Star Trek Next Generation*)
- Spock (from *Star Trek*)
- Sergeant "Just the facts Ma'am" Friday (from *Dragnet*)

Red Hat: The Emotional/Intuitive Hat

Focus: Exclusively on feelings, emotions, and intuition.

Questions

How do you feel about this?

What comes up for you when you think about this?

What does your intuition say about this?

What's your first impression about this?

What background feelings (positive or negative) do you bring to this discussion?

After hearing all that discussion and fully exploring the decision, what does your gut tell you to do?

Key Descriptive Phrases

- The emotional landscape
- The emotional filter for all your thinking on this subject
- Makes the subterranean emotional landscape explicit
- All feelings are simply accepted as a piece of the map
- Your final decision maker

Three Ways Emotion Influences Thinking

1. Background feeling (such as fear, disappointment, love, pride, anger)
2. Initial perception or reaction
3. Concluding feelings that prompt decision and action

Key Points

- Share Red Hat feelings *without* explanation or justification.
- Everyone *must* participate when a mastermind group goes to the Red Hat.
- All decisions boil down to Red Hat decisions.

Model Red Hatters

- Counselor Troy (*Star Trek Next Generation*)
- Oprah
- Leo Buscaglia

Black Hat: Your Bodyguard

Focus: Exclusively on what is wrong or could go wrong. This is the hat that deals with cautious risk assessment and wants to protect you from pain. It cares most about survival and keeping you safe by looking for what's wrong. This is the traditional western critical thinker. It anticipates obstacles and kills bad ideas before they get you into trouble.

Questions

What is wrong here?

What could go wrong?

How could this come back to haunt you?

What are the risks here?

How would a skeptical thinker see this proposal?

Key Descriptive Phrases

- Skeptical skeptic
- Applying the breaks
- Devil's advocate

Two Main Pitfalls

1. Using this hat too much!
2. Using the Black Hat as an excuse to argue.

Purpose

- To stop you from doing something stupid, costly, or painful.
- Lay out the landmines and pitfalls on the map so that you can plan how to avoid or mitigate them.
- Push you to come up with even better solutions and clearer thinking.

Three More Key Points

1. It's *not* about winning an argument . . . it's about laying out the dangerous parts to the landscape.

2. Always logical and not emotional (otherwise it's under the Red Hat).

3. Parallel Thinking is critical with the Black Hat. If people have conflicting Black Hat ideas, simply put both down and move on.

Model Black Hat Thinkers

- An attorney you are consulting with
- A police officer on patrol
- A bodyguard escorting you

Yellow Hat: The Enthused Champion

Focus: Exclusively on how to make an idea work and looking for what is good about a specific situation. Sensitized to see hidden opportunities and powerful leverage points. Searches out value and merit. Seeks out opportunity, solutions, and improvements.

Questions

How can we turn this around?

What's good about this?

Where's the seed of an equivalent or greater benefit here?

How can I improve on this idea?

How can I solve this problem?

How can this help us?

Key Descriptive Phrases

- Positive spin
- Pearl hunter
- Overwhelming desire to make things happen
- Passionate believer
- Source of boundless energy

Two More Key Points

1. Dig for breakthrough benefits and leverage opportunities that aren't so obvious at first. We are habitually too quick to settle for the first tangible solution we think of, and too slow to let go of good ideas to make room for great ideas.

2. It's *not* rah, rah emotional cheerleading (that's Red Hat). Yellow Hat thinking is supported by logical thinking. It focuses all your

positive, practical, energy on building creative solutions to make ideas work.

Model Yellow Hatters

- Zig Ziglar
- Tony Robbins
- Norman Vincent Peale

Green Hat: Your Creative Genius

Focus: Exclusively on new ideas and creating possibilities and new combinations and mixtures. The focus is on using ideas to move you to other new and novel ideas. It's about creating more and more options.

Questions

What are some totally new ideas to try out here?

What if . . . ?

Brainstorm all the potential ideas.

If I had a magic wand, what would the perfect solution look like?

Key Descriptive Phrases

- Novel ideas, combinations, and possibilities
- Creating options
- Flexibility
- Generation
- Out of the box
- Crazy ideas

A key distinction between Yellow Hat and Green Hat is that Yellow Hat thinking is about finding a useful idea or solution that is often based on improving an existing idea. Green Hat thinking is about creating something new, whether it's useful or not. Yellow Hat thinking is about utility; Green Hat thinking is about the raw generation of new ideas to explore where these ideas take you.

The Role of Provocation

Provocation is what gets Green Hat thinking going. It's the little stone that triggers an avalanche of ideas. Provocation is *not* argument or debate. Provocation means that you have an idea that it is different from what you normally thought that triggers a whole series of new, breakout ideas.

It's not a case of yes or no; the answer is purple. That's what provocation does. An example of provocation used in a positive way is the technique of reversal.

Reversal occurs when you take a normally accepted concept and reverse it with a "What if . . ." Then, with your Green Hat on, come up with the new ideas that are triggered.

For example, if you're concerned that the market for your business product or service is flooded with competition and there just isn't room for you to grow and expand your business profitably, you could put on your Green Hat and ask yourself a reversal question. You could ask, "What if we locked the doors and didn't allow any new clients into our business unless they got one of our current clients to 'sponsor' them? What would that look like?" Or you could ask yourself, "What would happen if we tripled our prices and fired at least 50 percent of our current customers?" As you can imagine, both these questions would stretch your thinking and help you generate novel ideas. That is the real purpose of the Green Hat.

Model Green Hat Thinkers

- Picasso
- Da Vinci
- Steven Spielberg

For Both Yellow and Green Hat

In most cases, there is rarely one best answer or solution. So, why settle for the one answer or solution you come up with just because it comes to mind first? The real value of *both* Yellow and Green Hat thinking comes when you push past the easy and obvious answers, ideas, and proposals.

Green and Yellow Hat thinking is often hard in our culture. We've been taught to think that decision making is the key step. Our culture emphasizes that the point of deciding is the ultimate decision point. Quality decisions don't come out of thin air. They are dependent on reviewing and expanding on quality *options*. This is why Yellow and Green Hat thinking is so critical and valuable for a Maui Millionaire. It might possibly be the single most important aspect of using a mastermind group to quickly leverage your time, talent, and money for the optimum results.

Our minds have a tendency toward logic. We want to explain things by labels. The term for this is "logical partitioning." Logical partitioning can be deadly to Green and Yellow Hat thinking. For example, if our business needs more income our thought might be that we have to (1) raise prices or (2) lower expenses. Our marketing department says we can't raise prices, so we conclude that we have to lower expenses. It's the logical partitioning that creates only two categories (or partitions) of answers. That limits the creativity and expansive thinking of Green Hat and Yellow Hat thinking. In reality there are limitless possibilities, not just two choices. We could introduce new products. We could phase out poorly performing services. We could license off a key technology. We could . . .

Let's use another example and assume you need more income. A better question might be, "How can I double my income by doing work that I love and believe in?" The Green Hat and Yellow Hat thinkers come alive with that type of question. It will take you to a completely different place.

Blue Hat: The Organizing Hat

Focus: Exclusively on the thinking process itself and how we are recording, organizing, harnessing, and putting to work the thinking we are doing. The blue hat is the hand that guides the focus of the thinking process—which hats to use and when, what questions to ask and how to frame the discussion, and how to create the action plan from the masterminding.

Questions

What is our purpose for this meeting?

What is the outcome you want from this area?

How are we defining the question or problem?

What are our specific next steps?

Who is responsible for them and by when?

How are they being held accountable?

Key Descriptive Phrases

- Conductor, choreographer, or facilitator
- Meta level thinking—thinking about how best to direct the thinking to accomplish the objective

The Three Main Phases of the Blue Hat Role

1. *At the start:* Frames the discussion and sets the focus, primarily through the use of a well-defined and designed question.
2. *During the process:* Records the results of the thinking (or sees that the results are captured) and reports/recaps/summarizes as needed.

3. *At the end:* Wraps the pieces together and gets clear on how the ideas will be converted into tangible results through the creation of a clear and powerful action plan.

Model Blue Hatters

- Captain Picard (*Star Trek Next Generation*)
- Colin Powell
- Abraham Lincoln

Harnessing the Power of the Six Maui Hats

The hats are merely tools. You don't need them all the time. You use them when you want to and put them away when they become too much. The hats work especially well if you feel your mastermind group bogging down. In a case like this, the facilitator may suggest that the group take a second and put on their Green Hats to brainstorm a question. Or the facilitator has everyone put on their White Hats and lay out the objective facts.

Remember the hats are about direction, not a specific destination. They are about influencing the way you are behaving and thinking. They are not labels you put on your thinking, in retrospect.

When you use a hat, make sure everyone wears the same hat at the same time. The only exception is for the facilitator. Usually you want to keep a facilitator wearing the Blue Hat.

Exercise Your Hat Muscle

Exercise 1: The Polarity Transformer™

Would you like to take an event that occurred in the past and change it? Well, you can't change what happened, but you can change how you think about it. The hats can help you do this quicker, with bigger results, than any other method. This is an exercise you can either do individually or as a group.

Think back on a bad result or painful event that you've had in your life.

Now, put your White Hat on and put the emotion aside. Take two minutes and write out what happened. Remember, you've got your White Hat on, so just the facts.

Draw a line on the paper. Put on your Red Hat and under the line, write out the meaning that you gave to the event. How did this event impact how you do business, make investments, or view relationships? In what other ways did it impact how you interact in the world?

After you've finished, draw another line. Put on your Yellow Hat. If you have a Yellow Hat, so much the better. If you don't, go through the motions of putting the hat on anyway. Remember the Yellow Hat is your enthused champion.

Now, with your Yellow Hat on, write out the lesson, insight, blessing, or gift that you received from this event.

If you have a member of your mastermind group available, recount the event and the gift that you received from it.

Question: So what did that event really mean?

Answer: Whatever meaning you chose to give it.

Exercise 2: An Exercise in Reversal

With your mastermind group, put your Green Hat on and for two minutes, quickly come up with ideas that are spurred by one of these reversal questions:

- What would happen if banks applied to you, so that you would be willing to accept their money?
- What if you had to build a million dollar business with no outside money—what would it look like?
- What if your business vendors and suppliers were your main company stockholders—how would this impact, change, influence, or revolutionize your business?

During that two-minute period, don't judge any idea. Remember the Green Hat doesn't accomplish anything. You don't create an action plan. It's not realistic. It's just about getting the ideas out there. People with little experience, and thus no so-called knowledge, often provide the greatest value here.

Now, put on your Red Hat and share your gut reaction to the ideas you generated. Do any of the ideas jump out at you as exciting, useful, or doable? How did creating these ideas change your perspective? Challenge your previous assumptions?

Exercise 3: The Hot Seat

This exercise is one that you might want to repeat more than once. At the Maui Mastermind wealth retreat, we call this the "hot seat."

Each member starts with the Blue Hat on. For two minutes each, write your thoughts to the following questions:

- What are the biggest challenges, obstacles, or opportunities that you face in your business or investing life right now?
- What are the biggest underutilized assets that you see that you have the potential to leverage that will allow you to achieve breakthrough results?

Now take a look at the thoughts that you've written. Pull them into one concise powerful question. An example might be, "How can I most effectively choose the right opportunities at the right time to maximize my income and minimize my time involvement?" Or, "How can I leverage my client base to double net profits in 12 months or less in a sustainable way?"

Next, the rest of the mastermind group puts their Green or Yellow Hats on. And then, in a rapid-fire method, they fire out answers to the question. Keep the answers short and the delivery in a shotgun matter.

Remember, just listen and record the ideas. You can figure out later how to implement the ideas and follow up with questions, but not now. For now, just listen and take in the flow of ideas.

There are a few hints to keep your mastermind group sessions on track during this process. Make sure you are very clear on the time given to each person and then stay true to the time. Use a timekeeper. Otherwise, the first few people will get all the time, and there will be no time left for the last few. You don't want to get in the habit of running long on your mastermind sessions either. You'll find people become too busy to take the time that way.

The Maui Hats in Everyday Life

The six Maui Hats are a powerful tool whenever you are dealing with tougher issues or are bogged down on a topic. If you have trouble making a decision, use the White Hat to gather the facts and perhaps the Yellow Hat to brainstorm solutions, but always use the Red Hat to make the ultimate decision. You'll notice that we didn't include the Black Hat in any of the exercises above. That's because we all get plenty of practice wearing the Black Hat. It's a valuable hat for its role, but it should be a minor role for the Maui Millionaire as he or she grows wealth in the best, most comprehensive way, with friends he or she really cares about.

David's Story

One use I've put the hats to in my business life is when I interview for new team members at any of my companies. The final interviewing team debriefs every final interview candidate using the following process. First, we put on our Blue Hats and review exactly what we are looking for. What type of person? What unique talents does the job require? What are the three to five critical competencies that the person we hire *must* have to succeed on a massive scale in this position?

Next we share a quick Red Hat check-in about our first impressions of the candidate so that we each know of any inherent biases or emotional associations the candidate may have triggered for us.

We then put on our Yellow Hat and talk about all the positive qualities the candidate possesses. We list out all the reasons he would be good to hire.

We follow this with a Black Hat session for all the shortcomings of the candidate. Why would he not be a good choice?

Finally, we put our Red Hats back on and score the person on a scale from 1 to 10 on the 3 to 5 key attributes or bottom lines of the position.

After we have done this process for our final three candidates the choice becomes easy and clear. What the hats do is allow us to avoid arguing and friction. Instead we all share the same frame and thinking style at the same time, and things work a whole lot better.

CHAPTER 14

How to Run a Mastermind Group to Guarantee Breakthrough Results

When you start putting your mastermind group together, remember that the most important key will be finding the right mix of people to invite to join you. Part of that will depend on what the focus of the group will be, but in almost every case make sure you choose people you find uplifting and positive to be around. Brainstorm a list of the possible people who you think would have good chemistry working together. You might have five people or you might have 50 people on your list. Don't worry, you'll narrow that list down as you actually talk with each person about doing a trial test run of a mastermind group. The ideal size for your mastermind group is probably somewhere between five to seven people. The larger the group, the harder it is to give everybody time in the spotlight during your regular mastermind meetings. But if the group is too small, you limit the scope of ideas and the synergistic combinations of wealth geometry.

As you start the mastermind group, commit to a trial period of eight to 10 working sessions together. Most times, that will mean approximately 90 days. At the end of the time, everybody gets a chance to check in to see how they felt the group worked. Agree up front that at the end of 90 days, anyone can opt out or change the group. There will be no hard feelings. It means it just isn't working the way it should. We suggest that you also all agree to communicate openly as a group along the way, so that there are no surprises for anyone at the end of your trial period.

There needs to be a focused, unifying theme so everyone can work together. You might want to have one mastermind group to work on charitable projects and another to work on business and financial success. It's difficult to combine different goals in one group unless there is one broader encompassing purpose. In general, it will be easier to start with one purpose that is shared by the group.

Set up a regular time to meet, at least on a monthly basis. We suggest weekly or bi-weekly. Be very clear as to the meeting time, and keep it the same. If your group is big, chances are there will be times when someone won't be able to make the date. However, all masterminders should agree that if there is a commitment to try out the group for a trial period, they need to make every effort to be at every meeting.

While it's more powerful to meet in person, this often isn't pratical. If you do most of your meetings via the phone, make sure you meet once a quarter or at least annually in person. And, include something fun while you do it!

One great way to do that is to make a commitment to attend the *Maui Wealth Weekends* that we host twice a year. These powerful two-day wealth workshops are not only a chance for you to get together in person with your mastermind group, but *all* of the proceeds from the event go directly to charity so you can feel good that you're using your money to help yourself and other people!*

> ### Setting Mastermind Group Expectations
>
> - Be very specific about expectations within the mastermind group.
> - Write out expectations so there are no misunderstandings.
> - Regularly check in to make sure expectations are being met.

---

*For more detailed information on how you can attend these semi-annual wealth retreats just go to **www.MauiMillionaireBook.com** and click on the "Live Events" tab. You'll also learn how you can leverage the weekend by networking with other wealth builders.

Running Your Mastermind Meetings

Someone needs to be the facilitator, and someone will need to be the timekeeper. It's best if initially these roles rotate. You will likely find that some people just naturally are better at the roles than others. Once everyone has taken a turn, if someone really likes doing one of the roles and is great at it—let them.

Use a conference calling service for the phone calls. Set up a conference line for the same time so that it's easy for everyone to stay in contact.

Divide up the available time for the mastermind group session so that everyone gets time to be spotlighted. One of the problems with mastermind groups occurs when the first people get more time and attention than the last. Bad feelings can start to grow when members get different levels of attention. A good, impartial timekeeper can take care of all of those problems.

Let's say you have eight mastermind group members and one hour to meet. Figure five minutes for the introductions, six minutes each to get the group's focused attention, and then a final five to seven minutes to conclude.

Always start on time and address the issue of any member who is late more than once or twice. The time is too tight to allow perennial latecomers and a casual attitude will soon infect your group.

One of the questions that you'll have to address is how you handle couples. Do they get their time together or individually? We suggest you decide this one ahead of time, and set it as one of your expectations.

What's the Best Length of Time for a Meeting?

The more frequently your mastermind group meets, the shorter your sessions need to be. Let's say you want to have an accountability mastermind (just two people) to help you stay on track with your daily exercising. This is a mastermind group that would meet for just a brief check-in on a daily or weekly basis. If your mastermind group meets once a week, you might want to run for one hour. If it's monthly, go for 90–120 minutes. One warning, though. It can be difficult to go more than 90 minutes on the phone. A better solution might be to break the mastermind group into two chunks. For example, if you need a two-hour mastermind group, go for an hour, take a 30-minute break, and come back for the second hour.

> **Seven Tips for More Effective Mastermind Sessions**
>
> 1. While you want like-minded individuals for the group with respect to a shared commitment to the mastermind group process, balance this with your desire for diversity. Different backgrounds and expertises lead to more powerful masterminding.
>
> 2. Establish the unifying focus.
>
> 3. Set a regular meeting time (such as every Tuesday at 9–10 A.M. EST, first Wednesday of every month at noon–1 P.M. PST, and so forth).
>
> 4. Determine the format for your meetings.
>
> 5. Agree to speak the truth, and do it respectfully.
>
> 6. Start with a trial period.
>
> 7. Check in regularly to make sure everyone is having his or her needs met.

Using the Hot Seat to Generate Breakthrough Ideas

The Hot Seat is a mastermind group technique that allows each member to get lots of possible solutions to her most important or pressing challenge or opportunity. It's a fun free-for-all that comes up with a boiling sea of possible answers. Some might not work, but all it takes is one powerful answer to make a huge difference. Each member will get to bring one question to the group and be on the Hot Seat as the possible solutions flow. Here's how it works.

The Hot Seat answers will only be as good as the questions you ask. Prior to the meeting, ask all participants to come up with their *Power Question*. One format for doing this is to recommend that each member take two to three minutes to write out all the ideas that come from considering one or both of the following questions:

What are the biggest challenges, problems, or opportunities you have in your business?

What are the most underutilized assets or resources that you have, and how can you best leverage them?

Likely you'll have several themes running through your answers. For example, let's say you feel overwhelmed with all the business opportunities people are showing you. A good question might be "How can I most effectively choose the right opportunities at the right time to maximize my income and minimize my time involvement?"

Power Questions

An answer is only as good as the question. Here are some sample Power Questions that we've heard in the past:

What are 20 or more ways that I can best leverage my resources to powerfully and joyfully create the life of my dreams?

How can we joyfully grow our marriage by better supporting each other's dreams?

How can we raise $1 million for this worthy purpose in 24 months in a healthy and fun manner?

How can I healthfully become and maintain my weight at 150 pounds and enjoy it for a lifetime?

How can I triple my passive income in 36 months in a balanced and sustainable way?

You've said what you want (choose the right opportunities at the right time) and given the parameters (maximize income and minimize time). You'll notice that we added in the element of qualifying our questions so that we "enjoyed the process" or "created more free time" or did it in a "healthy manner." It's always important to frame your question so that it supports what you *really* want to have happen. Any fool can work hard and get rich. The trick is to get wealthy and become a Maui Millionaire so that you can enjoy the Maui lifestyle too.

Remember your hats as you're running your mastermind group meeting. Start with a check-in with the Red Hat. This is a way to get in tune with each other and come together as a circle to close out the outside world. It's special because this is a sacred time that you dedicate to the fulfillment of a specific purpose.

With Red Hats on, each person checks in for 30 to 60 seconds on how he or she is feeling.

With White Hats on, check in on what the commitments were, what progress was made on those, and the three biggest developments since the last meeting. The key to making this work smoothly is to have everyone write this part out ahead of time. Remember it's the White Hat. Don't talk about how you feel about it or make any comments. It's just the facts!

Divide up the remaining time for all participants to go on the Hot Seat. You should have a facilitator and a timekeeper for your meeting.

If you're on the Hot Seat, here are some rules to get the most out of the experience:

- Listen carefully, and look for the nugget of an idea you can take away.
- Do not argue or explain.
- Never question the intent of the solutions you receive.
- Do not plan the strategies to implement (that's a later step).
- Have fun.

If you're generating ideas for the person on the Hot Seat, put on your Green or Yellow Hat and keep the ideas short. They should come out in a shotgun fashion—blast after blast. The solutions don't need to be practical and you don't need to figure out how to implement them now. Just let the ideas flow and grow as the group gets going with powerful, supersized answers.

After everyone gets a turn on the Hot Seat, you may want to include a Blue Hat moment. If you have time for this in the agreed-upon schedule, then everyone should come up with very clear action steps to put one or more of the ideas generated into action.

The final step of your mastermind group meeting should be a Red Hat moment. This is a great time for everyone to just check in again for 30 to 60 seconds on how they are feeling.*

Preparation for a Hot Seat Session

Each mastermind group member should do the following prior to the meeting:

- List out what your commitments from the last meeting were, what progress you made on those, and the three biggest developments since the last meeting.

- Sculpt a powerful question from the breakout thoughts that occur as you personally brainstorm the following questions:

  What are the biggest challenges, problems, or opportunities you now have in your business or investments?

  What are the most underutilized assets or resources that you have and how can you best leverage them?

---

*Would you like more ideas to use with your mastermind teams so that you can leverage your mastermind group to create even bigger results? Then go to **www.MauiMillionaireBook.com** and click on the "Mastermind" tab. You'll find dozens of proven ideas to help you mastermind more effectively including a FREE online workshop that will teach you exactly how to launch your own mastermind group right away!

Five Common Myths About Masterminding

1. "Argument leads to creation." *Fact:* Argument destroys the creative process.

2. "Creativity means no rules or structure." *Fact:* Structure gives creativity a framework in which to grow.

3. "I'll get more done on my own." *Fact:* You have no leverage when you have to do it all yourself.

4. "It's too much work." *Fact:* Get the right people on board, and the work becomes fun.

5. "We should always focus on achieving and doing. Forget this process stuff." *Fact:* We will be remembered more for the way we do things, and the lives we touch in the process, than we will be for the things we've achieved. The power is in the process.

Your mastermind group can be the most powerful tool that you have for creating wealth in a synergistic way. It will help you achieve all your dreams faster and with less effort and more fun. It's one important way we can all put the humanity back into wealth building. Let's move on to the seven most important wealth secrets that will enable you to harness the real power of your mastermind group.

CHAPTER 15

The Seven Most Important Wealth Secrets of a Mastermind Group

People can change their lives in relatively short periods of time. In fact, within six months after one year's Maui Mastermind, 90 percent of the attendees who said their goal was to leave their jobs and replace their earned income with passive income had indeed quit their jobs. They now invest full-time in businesses or real estate.

It might be hard to make that first phone call to start your mastermind group. And, once you're together, there might be a feeling of, *What do we do now?* The mastermind system works, but it will take some perseverance to keep it going. Here are some of the wealth secrets that we've discovered as we've grown our businesses through the help of mastermind groups.

The mastermind concept works and it can provide amazing results if you take the time and effort to set it up right. The rewards are there! Let's look at the seven most important wealth secrets of a mastermind group.

Mastermind Secret One: You Are Only One Mastermind Group Away from Having Everything You Ever Wanted

What would it be like to have true power in your life and all of your ventures? Can you imagine what it would be like to be part of a group of people that act with passion and purpose to take whatever dream you have and make it come true in an even bigger way than you thought possible?

That's what happens when you bring together sincere people who are committed to making dreams come true and have demonstrated that they have an ability to act—not just talk about something. If you surround yourself with successful people who are willing to take action, you can't help but do the same! You know you have a good mastermind group when you have to run to keep up.

A Mastermind Group That Made Some Dreams Come True

During a past Maui Mastermind, the participants were asked to write down their biggest dreams. And then they handed those pieces of paper in. What they didn't know was that a special mastermind group was formed in a different room, with the express purpose of selecting four of those dreams to make them come true on the spot.

Now, here's the secret that no one outside the room knew.

This special mastermind group had three hours to make four dreams come true, but it actually spent the first two hours playing around! Then, in the one hour remaining, they opened up their Rolodexes and started making calls. In less than one hour, four dreams had come true.

When you put a room full of people with strong connections together and ask them a powerful question, you will get not just one, but a series of powerful answers. And the answer is even bigger than you thought it could be.

How would you like to have full access to everyone *we* know? Do you think that if we sat down together for an hour, or a day, and you shared your biggest dream—that we might know just the person who, with one phone call, could open up all the doors that you had been banging your head against previously? That's the power of a mastermind.

You are quite literally one mastermind group away from having everything you've ever dreamed of. And the ultimate irony is that it is so easy to achieve when you are around the right caliber of people. It's so easy for them to connect you with one business owner, one lender, one expert, that can literally make you a million dollars in 90 days or less.

Mastermind Secret Two: Your Answers Depend on Your Questions

The answers we get in our life all depend on the questions we ask. We ask other people questions, and we ask ourselves questions. We're taught that there is no such thing as a dumb question. But, is that really true?

Some questions might not necessarily be dumb, but they could be very harmful. Perhaps a better way to put it is that the way we've been taught to ask questions is ineffective.

If you ask yourself, *Why can't I grow my business and profit margins?* You'll discover all the reasons that support the belief that you can't grow your business and your profit margins. The worst part is that even if there are ways to grow your business and profits, you'll eventually stop looking and instead become one of those dream killers who dissuade others from living their life to the fullest.

Three Steps to Powerful Questions

KEY CONCEPT

Step #1: Determine what it is that you really want.

Step #2: Ask yourself: Do the questions you habitually ask yourself and others support these goals?

Step #3: Now, supersize the questions you ask.

How can you turn an ordinary question into a powerful question? A powerful question spurs the person answering it to come up with ideas that are bigger than you ever envisioned. You never know how good an answer can be until you ask the right question.

Mastermind Secret Three: You Hold the Answer to Someone Else's Prayers

Have you lived up to the best that is in you? We all have the ability to create the life we want, and that is usually more than just creating a lot of money. In fact, that's the difference between a typical millionaire and a Maui Millionaire. A Maui Millionaire's life has room in it for other people.

If living up to your full potential isn't enough reason for you to decide to become a Maui Millionaire, then consider what it might mean to someone else. Think about it. What would happen to your family and your community if you didn't live up to everything you could be?

 Diane's Story

I'd like to share a deeply personal story with you. It's how my family changed because of a mastermind group.

The Maui Mastermind event started in 2003 during a meeting of my own personal mastermind group. The whole concept of the Maui Mastermind began because one of my mastermind partners kept pushing me with questions to find out what I really wanted. What did I love most about teaching? If I could create the perfect event, what would it look like? Who would I allow to come?

The answers flowed easily. I loved most teaching people who actually took action and put the ideas I shared into practice improving their financial life. The perfect event would be an extended event over five days in a beautiful location where we could really dive deep into the details of wealth. And the only people I would allow to come were positive, proven doers who were committed to living the life of their dreams.

The end result was the creation of Maui Mastermind—the world's most exclusive wealth retreat where a select handful of entrepreneurs, investors, and wealth builders come each year prepared to make quantum leaps in their lives.

(continued)

Diane's Story *(continued)*

One very important component to Maui that David and I built in from Day 1 was to use the event as a vehicle to raise money for worthy causes. And, in the spirit of a mastermind group, we asked all the Masterminders to come up with their suggestions of charities. That was Maui 2003, and from that one event we were able to give over $100,000 to charities around the world. Rob, one of the Maui Masterminders, had suggested an orphanage in Juarez, Mexico. We knew that the money was sorely needed due to some problems with their current building, but we didn't know the extent of it. A few months later, our event coordinator, Amy DeMeritt, called up the recipients to inquire about the impact that had been made by the gifts of Maui. When Amy spoke with the director of the orphanage, Sergio, Amy was blown away.

There was a property dispute, and they were going to get evicted from their current building. Sergio didn't want to ruin the kids' Christmas and so he let them celebrate the holiday without telling them. His plan was to tell them at the end of December that the orphanage was shutting down. Chances were that most of the kids would then be living on the streets, separated and abandoned again.

The check for $10,000 from Maui Mastermind arrived on December 26th. It was enough for them to get the building started. The children moved into the facility immediately, even though there wasn't yet a roof or a kitchen. At least they still had a home.

The impact on the kids was even more significant. They had grown up believing they weren't anything special. Now, they had tangible evidence that sometimes prayers do come true.

I never knew that the actions I took might create the answer to someone else's prayers. Amy and I were so moved that we cancelled a shopping trip to Europe and used that freed-up, long weekend to instead go down to Juarez to do a short film on the orphanage and meet Sergio. A little trip turned into a larger expedition, and my husband joined me.

(continued)

Diane's Story (continued)

We spent two days in Juarez. While there, we first visited an orphanage run by a lady named Mari Cruz. She took in girls, ages 11 to 16 years old, who had been all working the streets of Juarez as prostitutes. Most had drug problems as well. It felt good to fill up their cupboards and freezers with food to last the next few months.

We visited *Casa de la Nueva Vida* (House of the New Life) the next day. We brought some of the items they had on their wish list (meat, fruit, and inner tubes for their bicycle tires) and filmed a video. One teenage boy was so smart and articulate that it just made you wonder, *What on earth is he doing here?* At age 14, the chances were he'd soon be working in a factory, 12 hours a day, 6 days per week. He had the dream of being a doctor, but there was little chance of that happening. Something happened for my husband and me when we met this handsome, caring boy. And, that's why, at the end of the first day in Juarez, Richard said, "Let's adopt David."

Six months later, we brought our 14-year-old son from a Mexican orphanage to his new Phoenix home. I'd say that day was the happiest day of my life, but it's not true. Every day is the happiest day of my life, as I'm amazed at how much I love being a mom to David.

Sometimes the answers you get are to questions you didn't even know you had.*

*Would you like to see the actual video footage of the orphanages down in Juarez, including how a small group of Maui Masterminders made a huge difference in the lives of these children? Then go to **www.MauiMillionaireBook.com** right now!

Have you lived up to the best in you? The best way to have your dreams come true is to make someone else's dreams come true.

Mastermind Secret Four: Most People Are Too Busy Earning a Living to Make Any Real Money

Your mastermind group is the single most effective way to create change, quickly, and with a high degree of certainty. That's because a mastermind group builds in accountability and healthy peer pressure to live your best and highest self. If you don't follow through and do what you said you would, you have to answer to the rest of the group.

It's more than that, though. You also have a built-in team to brainstorm with, to analyze business or investment deals with, to run ideas past, to search for new resources with, and, in general, to be there when you need it.

These are a few of the basic ideas why mastermind groups can create such amazing results for people. Now, let's get down to the bottom line. What does it take to create real wealth?

The real secret to wealth creation is to stop working. Let me say it another way. The secret is to stop working the way you've been doing it. Most people trade time for money. In fact, highly-paid professionals such as doctors might make a lot of money, but if they stop working—the money stops, too.

The problem with trading your time for money is that you have to watch your expenses to build wealth. Face it, there are two ways to have more money left over after you've paid all your bills: (1) make more money, or (2) cut your expenses.

Most people have been taught that the only way to surely have money is to cut expenses. That's because they believe their ability to make money is limited.

If you want different results, you'll need to look at expenses in a totally different way. For example, money spent that makes your business or investments work better, is an investment—not an expense.

The biggest question then is, "What is the return on your investment?"

That brings us to one other asset you have that most people take for granted. It's the most precious asset you have because it's the one asset that is limited. You can make more money. Shoot, with the techniques we discuss in this book and that you'll perfect with your mastermind group, you have lots of income potential. But this other asset just can't be increased. What is it? It's your time. Where you invest your time is one of your highest expressions of what you choose to have your life be about.

You owe it to yourself, to your family, and to the future you envision not to waste it. Make sure the mastermind group you form and the investments in people, relationships, businesses, real estate, and paper assets are worth your time investment. So, before you agree to another time commitment, ask yourself, *What is the return on this prospective investment of my time and life energy?*

And, perhaps, scariest of all—why spend your time building someone else's dream? Build your own. Stop working so hard and start making real wealth.

The secret to maximizing your wealth potential is leverage. And that leads to Mastermind Secret Five.

Mastermind Secret Five: Leverage Can Work in Every Area of Your Life to Create More Powerful Results with Less Effort

Leverage is the ability to do more with less. It's also the secret behind most great fortunes. For example, one Maui participant leveraged a single business outlet into over 75 offices around the country. Another Maui graduate used $7.5 million of borrowed money to buy a commercial property that he sold roughly a year later for $9.6 million.

But, don't stop there. You have the ability to leverage not only money but also time, talent, knowledge, databases, and Rolodexes. Your mastermind group can provide all of these resources and help you create ways to leverage them.

The fastest, easiest way to program yourself for great wealth is to immerse yourself in a mastermind relationship with other successful people!

Look for people who are earning more than you are, who are living a fuller life and enjoying it even more . . . then fight like crazy to deserve to be part of that group.

Mastermind Secret Six: The Real Secret to Making Money Is . . .

We're on to Secret Six, the Holy Grail of investments and business. What is the real secret to making money?

It's letting go of your old stories and unleashing your freedom to choose fresh what your life means.

We have a free society with economic conditions that are unparalleled in our history. We should all be rich. Yet we aren't. What is stopping you from living up to your fullest potential? What do you need to remove from your life that is stopping you from having all you want?

What belief is holding you back? What do you think about money or your right to have it?

One year at Maui, one of the Maui Guest Stars, Beverly Sallee, shared her belief about money, which was that you should make as much money as you can so that you have more to give away to do good in the world. Well, this impacted many participants, including Stephen. In fact, this one idea completely transformed how he thought about wealth. Stephen had always believed, down deep, that something was wrong with making money. This new belief was very freeing. He discovered that he could contribute to the world by making a ton of money, and sharing that money with the world in healthy, positive ways.

Jeff, another Maui Millionaire, shared with us how powerful it was for him to be able to share with his mastermind group that he was a millionaire. He said he hadn't been able to tell anyone else in his old circle of friends that he was a millionaire. He said he couldn't tell anyone because he was afraid they would want something or negatively judge him.

Too often, we've been conditioned to believe that we can't have, that we don't deserve, that we aren't smart enough, that we don't work hard enough . . . or, well, you fill in the blank. It's whatever stupid lesson someone else tried to foist off on us. You don't need those beliefs. You *do* deserve the wealth you create. It doesn't take money to make money. Surround yourself with people who have the beliefs you know will enrich your life and make you bigger—not smaller.

The only thing that is stopping you from achieving and enjoying your heart's desire is your old, outdated story of why you can't have it.

Mastermind Secret Seven: The Most Powerful Skill You Can Develop Is to Learn to Act in the Presence of Fear

Every time you work outside your comfort zone, you will be in an unknown territory. It will be a little (or a lot) frightening. What will you do at that moment? Once you've had a glimpse of what is possible, you can never go back to the same life.

You have a choice. You can either move forward, face the fear, and take a huge step into the great unknown. Or you can shrink back, hoping for the old security, but never be quite satisfied in what you have settled for.

The choice is up to you. What will you do when you are presented with a great deal or business opportunity? Will you go for it or let fear stop you? Use your mastermind group as a support system to help you grow your comfort zone and take consistent action toward making your big dreams come true.

Now What?

You've learned how to set up and run a mastermind group, and you've reviewed the seven wealth secrets of a mastermind group. Are you maximizing the potential within your group? It won't always be easy. Sometimes, day-to-day life will get in the way of people living up to their commitments. Plus, you will often have to work to balance the time needed for each person, so that each member has her needs being met. But, if you go the extra mile to create and maintain a powerful mastermind group, you may just find that this section has actually been the most important key to your becoming a Maui Millionaire.

Next, we'll turn our attention to the most powerful wealth model ever created.

PART FOUR

MAUI WEALTH LEVERAGE STRATEGY FOUR:
Build Level Three Wealth and Enjoy a Maui Lifestyle!

CHAPTER 16

How to Make Money Without Working

Money by itself doesn't necessarily lead to wealth. It's not enough to just make a ton of money; you need to build your wealth in such a way that it truly creates financial freedom. In this part, you'll learn The Five Wealth Factors™ and the secret Maui Financial Freedom Formula™. You'll even learn a breakthrough new system for measuring your *real* financial progress.

Now, however, it's time to talk about the financial strategies and models you need to build your financial wealth in a way that gives you time, freedom, and balance.

Think about it this way. There are three critical elements you are working to balance with your wealth building. First, there is your business life. These are businesses you own, run, or work in. Often these businesses are the active cash flow generators that you work in daily, like a consulting firm you own, or an Internet business you started, or even a large corporation that you work for. As you'll see, coming up, many Maui Millionaires got their start by using the active income their businesses generated to invest to create passive income for themselves.

Next, there is your investment life. This is where you take the cash you earn in your business life and invest it into assets that create more wealth for yourself. These investments don't just create cash flow, ideally they create passive, residual cash flow, like quarterly distributions that a passive business interest generates or the monthly cash flow from a commercial property.

Finally, there is your personal life. Maui Millionaires have learned to balance their businesses and investments in such a way that they support and enhance their life, never running or dominating it. Remember the proverb, "How does it profit a man to gain the world but lose his soul"? Well, we use this passage from the Bible to remind us that our business and investing efforts need to feed and support our life, never rule or control it, which leads us to a frank discussion of one of the key themes of being a Maui Millionaire: time freedom.

Time Freedom

Time freedom, one of the essential components to true wealth, comes not from the absence of things to do or commitments to meet. Rather it comes when we claim our God-given freedom to choose the things we want to do and to commit to the things that most matter to us. It is a freedom that is enhanced when you build your financial house the right way, and it is the essence of living a wealthy life.

Remember, Maui Millionaires have full plates and plenty to do. It's just that they choose what's important to them, and they set their own agendas. They are the ones who decide what to do and with whom they do it. Maui Millionaires know that life is too short and precious to waste on activities or people they don't enjoy.

It's important to understand that a big part of time freedom is having a great team to help you accomplish what matters most. For most Maui Millionaires this means that they have found world-class people to help them put and keep their financial worlds in order. These key team members might include a professional bookkeeper, office manager, executive assistant, or property-management company. Your team will also include financial professionals like a world-class CPA, attorney, insurance agent, mortgage broker, and real estate agent to help you freely navigate your financial landscape with less time, more safety, and better results.

Another big part of creating time freedom for yourself is developing the systems that let you free your mind and attention from the little things that would otherwise crowd out the big things. How do you organize your time? How do you capture ideas? What kind of tickler system do you have that makes sure that the right information comes to your attention at just the right time? If all this talk of systems and organizing yourself makes your head spin and your eyes bulge, then we suggest you consider leveraging an exceptional personal assistant to help you free up your time and handle many of the fine details of your life for you.*

Level Three Wealth—A Powerful Model for Creating True Financial Freedom

Over the past decade of building wealth ourselves and helping thousands of individuals lead richer, wealthier lives, we've developed a key distinction. Over time we've refined this distinction until it's reached its present form, which we call the Level Three Wealth Model™. In our opinion, it is almost impossible to be truly financially free without understanding and tapping into this powerful model, at least intuitively.

There are three levels of wealth. Level One is where you are just getting started. We call this level the Launch Stage. You enter Level One of your wealth building the moment you make a conscious and determined decision to become financially free. It's at this moment that a lifetime of wealth becomes a real possibility for you.

The goal of all Level One wealth builders is to reach the place where they comprehensively—intellectually, emotionally, and intuitively—know that it is possible for them to become financially free. The key distinction is that while many people believe that it is possible for *other* people to become financially free, Level One wealth builders are working to reach the point where they know it is possible for themselves. At this point in their wealth building, the financial vehicle they start with is almost immaterial, since the real leverage point for Level One wealth builders lies with their W.O.S. This is why Maui Millionaires all began their wealth building by consistently upgrading their W.O.S. In parallel with this work it's important for Level One wealth builders to begin building the basic skills of financial mastery.† In the next chapter, we'll

---

*To learn how to master Level Three effectiveness skills, including more about how to leverage a full or part-time assistant to make your life smoother, richer, and more enjoyable, just go to **www.MauiMillionaireBook.com**. While there, you'll even learn about how to protect yourself from the five pitfalls that create financial havoc that trip up most people who rely on outside financial professionals.

†Would you like to learn more about the Seven Foundational Wealth Skills of the world's wealthiest people? Just log onto **www.MauiMillionaireBook.com** and click on the "Online Workshops" tab to participate in these FREE online wealth workshops. For full details see the Appendix.

not only share with you the best investment focuses for Level One wealth builders, but we'll explain how your investment focus needs to change as you progress through Level Two and Three wealth building. For now, it's enough for you to understand that Level One wealth builders are working for the day when they realize that they can build wealth and become financially free. Yes, they also recognize that they still may have several years of work to get there, but they get it in their guts that it is a tangible possibility for them personally.

Level Two wealth builders are in the process of building up their wealth. They are focused on the mechanics of building their wealth including learning the core business, financial, and investor skills and strategies they need to build wealth. Level Two wealth builders are actively engaged—day to day—in building their wealth. At first, they are the sole drivers pushing their wealth-building enterprises forward, but later they start to tap into other people to help them grow their wealth. Eventually Level Two wealth builders are able to put the financial and business infrastructure in place so that they can step out of the day-to-day operation of their business or investments and step up to Level Three Wealth.

Level Three wealth builders have gone passive in their investing and become financially free. They now spend less than 10 hours per month overseeing any one of their investment or business income streams and still get to enjoy the consistent cash flow they generate—year after year. A Level Three business is one in which you no longer have to show up to run each day. Instead, you have built your company in such a way that other people are empowered to maintain and grow it. The business works without you having to be there to work it each day. Level Three investments are ones in which you truly stay in the passive investor role and don't have active involvement in the day-to-day operation of whatever you have invested in—whether it be a business interest or a commercial property.

At this point, we need to make one of our personal wealth-building biases very clear—we both have built the bulk of our wealth by building businesses and investing in real estate. One area we haven't used to build wealth has been through stocks of publicly-traded companies, bonds, and mutual funds. It's interesting to note that while many Maui Millionaires have temporarily parked a portion of their money in publicly-traded securities, most Maui Millionaires have *created* the real bulk of their wealth through building businesses and investing in real estate. Our take on this is that while publicly-traded stocks, mutual funds, and bonds may be the only option that average people see for themselves, rarely are they an accelerated way to wealth. While there is nothing wrong with slowly accumulating wealth over a 40-year working career, it's just that Maui

Millionaires have learned that if they focus their efforts to learn key strategies, they can build their wealth in half, a quarter, or even a tenth of the time.

We'll share with you some of these key strategies in the next few pages, but for now, what is essential for you is to understand that the reason why businesses and real estate offer such an opportunity for you is that with them you can ensure that you have meaningful control over your investments, be they a business or a property, in a way that you cannot with a publicly-traded security. We like real estate and businesses because we have developed the expertise so that we have an advantage when we move in these worlds to build wealth.

Maui Millionaires have all consciously cultivated this same wealth-generating advantage, so that they consistently earn enhanced returns with much less risk than the average wealth builder. Remember, it is a half truth that the greater the return the greater the risk. The full truth is that when you understand the business or market you are investing in, you can intelligently hedge your risks by taking prudent steps like performing detailed due diligence, securing top notch accounting and legal advise, and building fall-back options into your business or investment structure from the very beginning to minimize downside risks. Maui Millionaires have both the financial skills to intelligently evaluate and structure business opportunties, and they also have the courage to take action when the time is right.

Morgan's Story

When Morgan Smith was building his mortgage business he held onto the costly belief that he needed to be the one in control. As long as he held this belief, he was only able to grow that one branch of Morgan Financial. Quickly he, like other Maui Millionaires, learned that he couldn't grow without letting go of much of the oversight of the day-to-day operations of his business. In fact, what he came to learn was that there were people out there who were more talented than he was in operations and management. About this time, he found Aaron, one of his first key hires. Aaron was the first person Morgan really trusted enough to recruit and lead part of his sales force. And what a smart move that was! Aaron excelled when Morgan gave him clear direction and focus and then stepped out of his way.

(continued)

Morgan's Story *(continued)*

Fast forward 10 years. Now Morgan Financial has 45 "Aarons" on its team and has grown to 161 branches.

Recognize that most entrepreneurs start out with a great need for control. They fear that if they let go and lose this control, bad things will happen. But without learning to intelligently build and empower teams to get the day-to-day work done, no business can grow, and the entrepreneur will be trapped in a Level Two business forever. Remember, the only way to grow a Level Three business is to clearly build with the end in mind of stepping completely out of the day-to-day operation of the business.

It's by moving from Level One through to Level Three that you are able to build Level Three Wealth. This is the type of wealth that allows you to live the Maui lifestyle where you are the one in charge of what you do each day, and who you get to do it with. Level Three Wealth also means you have simplified your life so that you are consistently spending most of your energy with the people that matter most to you, doing things that you are passionate about, and building a legacy to leave behind to bless the lives of others. This is the real driver for almost all Maui Millionaires, and they carefully eliminate from their lives those petty frictions and trivial distractions that diffuse the energies of so many people in our society.

Why Every Business Owner Needs to Learn to Invest and Why Every Investor Needs to Learn to Build a Business

Have you ever seen that old commercial for Reese's Peanut Butter Cups? You know the one where through some accident someone's chocolate bar falls and lands in a jar of someone's peanut butter and they both discover that they go perfect with each other.

Well, business building and investing are like peanut butter and chocolate—two great things that work synergistically together.

Businesses are great to generate cash flow and quickly build equity, but they are harder to use to create secure, long-term, passive, residual cash flow. It takes a deft touch to build a business in such a way that you can turn that business into a thriving, growing, and passive business for you, the founder.

Investments are great to create cash flow, but for this cash flow to be passive and residual it often requires a healthy-sized pool of starting capital with which to fuel your passive, residual return. Are you starting to get a sense of why these two wealth vehicles fit so well together?

First, we want to talk with the business builders and entrepreneurs out there. We've both found that the easiest way to generate a *ton* of cash flow is to build a thriving business. No passive investment will ever generate the same amount of net cash flow for you that a well-run business you are actively growing will with the same investment of money. That's why we love businesses, and why over the past 25 years we've both created and built up dozens of businesses. When you combine your passion with a specific market opportunity, you are able to build a business that churns out cash flow.

But we've also come to learn that turning a thriving, active business into a passive, residual business is much harder than most people realize. It's easy to get into a business, but harder to work your way—profitably and *residually*—out of the business.

That's why it's so important that business builders take a percentage of their time and energy, and focus it on building a portfolio of assets that generate passive, residual income outside of the time they put into growing their business. Besides, since the most common exit strategy most entrepreneurs have is to sell their business for a cash price, they would do well to take the time to learn how to invest their money in real estate, which is one of the best ways to convert cash into passive cash flow in a safe, stable, and growing way.

A simplified picture of our basic wealth bias is to build a business to generate cash flow and to invest that excess cash flow into real estate. Your active business can be a web-based business, a real estate investing business, a professional services firm, or any of hundreds of businesses, but just make sure you are investing a portion of your excess profits into outside diversified investments that will generate passive, residual income for you and your family—ideally for generations to come.

David's Story

One of the businesses I built was an investor training and mentoring company. Over the years, that business generated millions of dollars of net profit for me, and I had a blast building it up. I got a positive charge by helping new investors succeed in real estate. But many days I was faced with the choice of putting my time to growing that business or taking the time to buy more real estate. I look back at how on many occasions I passed on great investment deals because I didn't want to take the time to set up the deal, which might only generate a tenth of the monthly income that the same energy focused on growing my business would have reaped. What I didn't see at the time was that there might be a day when I would walk away from that business. And, in fact, nine years after I started that business my partner Peter came to me and said he wanted us to end the partnership.

After several long heart to hearts, we agreed that he would buy me out of my half of the business. I walked away with a big chunk of cash for my interest, but it meant that I also would no longer get any share of the healthy cash flow from the business.

I often look back at key moments in my life and ask myself what I would do differently if I had the chance to live that moment over. For me, it's a way of distilling the key lessons from any life experience. In this area, one of the things I would do differently next time is that I would change my investing strategy as I began to accumulate a large net worth. Early on, it was the best thing I could do to focus all of my energies on building my business. But I didn't update that wealth strategy as my net worth shot up. In retrospect, I would have shifted away from looking for ways to invest my time, money, and energy for forced appreciation—which I had in the form of building my business and buying real estate such as single family houses for equity build up—to investing in more cash-flow-creating real estate such as commercial real estate and apartment buildings.

David's Story *(continued)*

My advice to anyone who owns a successful business? Start today to take a minimum 10 percent of your time and energy and begin to build a portfolio of high quality rental real estate, either residential or commercial as best meets your situation and desire, in solid areas with professional management in place.*
Not only will you be building up your passive, residual cash flow, but you will also be ready for the day you sell your business, if in fact you choose this as an exit strategy, and walk away with a large lump sum of money that you need to intelligently invest to create passive, residual income.

*Professional management may be an outside company you hire or an internal investing infrastructure that you build. If you would like to learn more about building a real estate investing business that works so you don't have to, go to **www.MauiMillionaireBook.com** and click on the "Real Estate" tab. Inside you'll find dozens of proven strategies and powerful investor resources. For full details see the Appendix.

Now, for those investors out there who either invest in other businesses or invest in real estate, we have one very important question to ask you: How can you ever intelligently understand a business or property you are investing in if you don't understand how businesses work? This is why we feel so strongly that every investor must also become a solid and skilled business person, too. Business is the medium in which every investment lives, breaths, and, far too often for the poorly trained, dies. This is why we feel that every investor benefits greatly from learning more and more business skills.

Diane's Story

My husband (Richard) works the opposite of many of my tax clients in my CPA practice. Most of my clients make their money through their businesses and then invest the proceeds in real estate. In my husband's case, he's been doing "fix and flips" in recent years, which is an active form of real estate investing. He then takes the money he makes and invests it in businesses.

Richard has a due diligence checklist before he invests in any business, which includes investing only in businesses that are already operating with proven track records or in start-ups where the operating managers have a lot of experience. He's had his share of dot-com-type successes of investments in companies that go public and make it big. But the investments that we like the best are the ones in smaller companies that create monthly cash flow.

One company like that is a real estate office. Richard invested as much as they'd let him invest in a start-up real estate office. In reality, he wasn't investing because of the business so much as he was investing in the broker who would run the company. The investment is completely passive, and each month we get a check equal to about 8 percent of the total investment. That's right—year after year, we get a return of almost 100 percent on the initial investment.

Investing in business can be just like investing in real estate. In this case, though, your assets will be people, systems, market position, and quality products or services to market.

Are you starting to see why Maui Millionaires use both businesses and investments to build their Maui Lifestyle? Then let's move on and dive into *The Five Wealth Factors* that will help you create the Maui Lifestyle.

CHAPTER 17

The Five Wealth Factors

There are five Wealth Factors that cumulatively determine your real financial wealth. Let's walk through each of these five Wealth Factors in turn and see how you can use this understanding to speed you on your way to becoming a Maui Millionaire.

Wealth Factor One: Cash Flow

Cash flow is the money that flows to you. This could be a paycheck, an owner's draw, a check at the closing when you sell a property, or a quarterly distribution from a passive partnership. The distinguishing feature to this form of wealth is that it is liquid money—cash—that comes to you.

There are three main types of cash flow that we're interested in at the moment:

1. Earned income, also known as *active* cash flow.

2. Passive cash flow.

3. Passive *residual* cash flow.

Earned Income

Earned income is active cash flow that you work for day after day. Most people's main source of wealth comes from earned income, whether this be wages or salary that they earn from working a job or net profit that they generate from running a business. Please understand one very important fact. You will almost never become wealthy from earned income alone. Why not? Because the way our culture works is that the more you work and earn in the form of earned income, the harder it is for you to become financially free from just this source of income alone.

Diane's Story

I've spent over 25 years as a CPA advising business owners and real estate investors on how they can legally pay a whole lot less in taxes than they do right now.

That was why Neil and Mary came to me to begin with. Neil was a highly successful doctor in Florida. Mary liked to keep active and so wanted to keep working. She worked part time as a nurse. Neil didn't want to work forever, so he'd started to invest in apartment buildings.

That's when I first met them. They had a very high income, primarily from Neil's medical practice, and they also had some great tax write-offs from their apartment buildings. The problem was that they couldn't take the tax write-offs.

You see, the tax code actually punishes you if you make too much money in earned income. You're limited in how much you can take in real estate deductions against earned income.

There was one loophole, though. (A loophole is a government incentive to promote public policy.) If either Neil or Mary would become a full-time real estate professional, they would be able to take all the write-offs. That meant that one of them would have to spend more time in real estate activities.

(continued)

Diane's Story *(continued)*

So, the only way for Neil and Mary to start getting the benefit of their tax savings strategies was if someone quit their job! Mary quit and started becoming more involved with the real estate. As a result, they bought more properties. Now, here's the truly amazing part. In less than three years, Neil and Mary had more income from their real estate then they had from both Neil and Mary's earned "working" income before.

The only way they could start building wealth, and pay less tax, was to quit working so hard. Pursuing earned income just kept them on the treadmill, it didn't make them rich.

Earned income is like sugar. It gives you a jolt of energy but leaves you feeling empty and tired. Earned income comes in and out of your life so quickly that it often makes it *harder* to become wealthy. We know this is counterintuitive, but still we've observed this in the lives of many of the people who've come to us for coaching to become wealthy.

Here is the sad cycle we've observed build up and repeat in so many people's lives. They focus on getting the right job or profession so that they can earn a good salary (earned income). As they start to earn more they begin to spend more. In fact, not only do they spend on those nice little extras like a trip here or a meal out there, but they also spend on things that create a higher fixed cost of living. They buy a bigger house; they make payments on two or three nicer cars; they send their kids to expensive private schools. These are things that have payments due month after month, year after year. Once they acquire these things it is very difficult to ever stop paying for them. The higher their cost of living goes up, especially their fixed cost of living, the more they feel trapped in the rat race of working to support their lifestyle. They are forced to work long hours just to keep from falling too far behind.

We want you to imagine that earned income is like sugar. It tastes sweet but burns fast. It doesn't last. And in its wake it leaves you craving more. To get your next sugar fix, you're forced to go back to a job you don't love, to spend 8 to 12 hours with people you may not enjoy, come home tired and stressed, so that the next morning you can wake up and repeat the process.

Most people are addicted to sugar and living their life on a treadmill chasing after their next month's sugar.

Active Income is Sugar

"Income" is only Sugar!

The Earned Income Trap™

You will never become financially free from earned income alone!

It's Sugar...

The RAT Race!

Rats chase after Sugar!

The Rat Race!
You are forced to stay on the Treadmill.

You **spend** the money supporting a lifestyle — working hard to earn sugar...

Empty Calories!

The Solution?

Create other types of income & tap into the other 4 WEALTH factors!

And, if you can imagine that it's possible, things are actually even worse for those people who live off the sugar of earned income. It is the heaviest taxed form of income! This means that for every dollar you earn of earned income you are paying from 15 to 50 percent more tax than if it was another form of income.* This means you have to work even harder just to keep from flying off the back end of the treadmill. Is it any wonder so many people feel that the harder they work the further and further they are falling behind?

Think about the average high earner for a moment. They may earn $200,000 to $500,000 or more in income, but they end up paying 45 to 55 percent or more of this in taxes at the state and federal level. They tend to spend more than they earn supporting a lifestyle that has little or no enduring value, but has high fixed costs to maintain. They spend on things like big houses and fancy cars and impressive vacations. They live a life of instant gratification (also know as a fast high) where they live in a peer group of other spenders (also known as environmental pressure to use) where day by day they have to work harder and harder to maintain the lifestyle they no longer feel they have the time or energy to enjoy. Welcome to the rat race!

Remember, active income is just like sugar. It provides calories, but these are empty calories, that sustain people but don't nourish them. And like sugar, active income burns fast and is highly addictive. And as with any addictive substance, we start to build a tolerance for it—and continually spend more and more. Once the cycle can no longer be maintained, when a person no longer has the active income to support a lifestyle habit, there are massive withdrawal pains.

When you're living on the edge, addicted to sugar, scared to get off the treadmill for fear it will all come crashing down, you are caught in the rat race. If you're poor, then you struggle to survive, to just get through the day. If you're middle income, then you struggle to make ends meet each month. And if you're a high earner, you may be the king rat, but you have a hidden struggle to keep up appearances.

Understand this. If you *must* work to feed your lifestyle, then you are still in the rat race. There is a simple test to see where you currently stand. If you stopped working for income, would you still have the pas-

---

*Diane gets more into the tax strategies and consequences involved with different income sources as part of the Maui Millionaires Wealth Mentorship Program™ available to you at **www.MauiMillionaireBook.com**. Learn how the uninformed who live off of earned income actually spend their lives on a treadmill that the government turns up the dial, via taxation, to the hardest setting. Diane will share with you some foundational tax principles that will help you legally minimize your tax burden.

sive, residual cash flow to support your lifestyle? If the answer is no, then you are running in the rat race.

There is nothing wrong with the rat race. All Maui Millionaires started out there, but they all made a conscious commitment to escape as quickly as possible. And you can do the same thing. So what's the way out of the rat race? To invest and grow the other four wealth factors, and to cultivate healthier types of cash flow (aka passive cash flow and passive *residual* cash flow).

Maui Millionaires know how important it is to use active income to invest in accumulating the assets that generate the passive, residual income they need to support their lifestyle in a healthy way.

Here's the bottom line—Maui Millionaires know that earned income is only one of the five wealth factors, and in fact it is the least important. We hope you find this fact encouraging if you are on the front end of your wealth building.

Passive Cash Flow

It's time to talk about the next type of cash flow—passive cash flow. Passive cash flow is money that flows to you without your having to actively work to get it. Now with any investment it takes some time to set it up and to oversee it, so we have created the litmus test for whether or not a specific stream of income is passive or active. Passive cash flow is income that flows to you with your having to work less than 10 hours per month to maintain that income stream.

While that 10-hour limitation is arbitrary (we could have chosen 12 hours or 8 hours), it has come out of our personal experiences building wealth and coaching other people to build great wealth.

Your goal is to generate enough passive cash flow so that you never have to work again. When you reach this place, you now are financially free. Chances are you'll still work, but you'll do this out of choice and freedom not out of constraint and desperation.

Diane's Story

I started out my career as a typical CPA. I worked very long hours, especially during tax season. I made approximately $60,000 per year. It was a decent wage back when I first got into practice, but I worked very hard for it. In fact, I was burned out and wanted to sell my practice. Not only was I exhausted, but I watched a whole group of my peers go through very painful declines.

The problem was that even after I had sold my first CPA practice I still felt the passion to help people achieve financial freedom, and I knew how to help people save 50 percent or more on their taxes.

The answer for me was to start a business again, but this time run it so I only did the things I felt passionate about and that I was highly effective at. I would find other people who were passionate about the other things. One of the things that became really obvious was that there was a basic lack of financial literacy and tax literacy, and so I launched a web site (www.taxloopholes.com) that provided new weekly tax strategies and information about building wealth in the best tax-advantaged way. I also started writing books, something I had dreamed of doing since I was a little girl. I spoke at seminars in exciting locations around the world with mentors I had long admired. My life was exciting, and it didn't feel much like work anymore, when I did work! And, to be perfectly honest, I often didn't work for months at a time.

Now here is the amazing thing. I make five to seven times what I used to earn from my business with a fraction of the time, energy, and effort! I had to stop working so hard at making earned income so that I could concentrate on ways to create passive income that flows to me whether I work or not.

A Simple Story That Explains the Fundamental Secret of the World's Wealthiest People

Most of you will remember the old folk tale of the goose that laid the golden egg. It seems there was this farmer who one morning made the incredible discovery that one of his geese had laid a golden egg. He took in his precious discovery to show his wife who hovered over him as they weighed their valuable egg. To the delight of both of them, the next morning their amazing goose produced another golden egg.

Well, this grew to be a regular occurrence, with the goose producing one single golden egg each morning. Finally, the farmer's wife grew upset with waiting for that stingy goose to give them only that one egg each day. So she convinced her husband to butcher the goose and get all the golden eggs in one fell swoop. And reaching for his ax, that is exactly what the farmer did. Only to his and his wife's dismay, they found that once the deed was done there were no more eggs inside the goose at all. We like to think of this as a metaphor describing one of the key lessons for wealth builders: If you are investing solely for capital gains, then you are investing by fattening up and slaughtering your goose. This may work to eat well for one fine meal, but to eat over the long term you would do better to gather the eggs month after month, year after year.

So what is the difference between investing for capital gains and investing for residual cash flow? Well, capital gains comes when you sell an asset you own. And as you can figure out, once you sell something you no longer are able to sell it again or use it to earn ongoing income. Residual cash flow, on the other hand, are things like quarterly disbursements of profits from a business partnership, or monthly cash flow from an investment property. It is something you get again and again and again, provided the goose (read asset) is properly fed and cared for. One way to see your role in building wealth is that of a breeder and caretaker of golden geese.

Why It Isn't Enough to Create Passive Income

David's Story

One of the most important wealth lessons I learned happened after 10 years of my investing for forced appreciation and equity growth. Over that time, I had made a lot of money from the sale of properties I had in my real estate portfolio. Now, I had set up my real estate business to be a passive business for me by partnering up with various other people on different properties. This meant when we sold a house and split a $200,000 profit, my share of profits was passive income for me, since I didn't have to do much work to earn it. And because we had held onto those properties over 12 months we also benefited by only having to pay long-term capital gains taxes. And for a decade I was satisfied with this formula. What I've come to realize, however, is that once one of these properties was sold, I never made any more money from that property again.

(continued)

David's Story *(continued)*

Yes, the checks were quite nice from selling off a number of homes each year, but by that point I realized I didn't need the large lump sums of money. In fact, I really wanted residual cash flow instead. It was at this point that I learned the difference between investing for capital gains and investing for cash flow. When you invest for capital gains you are butchering your golden goose for a large surplus of meat. I've come to realize that I prefer a steady stream of golden eggs to a lump sum of golden goose flesh.

Now don't get me wrong, I'm not saying that investing for capital gains is wrong. In fact, the opposite is true. In the early and middle stages of your wealth building, if you want to build wealth fast, you should be focused on using forced appreciation to help you increase your net worth and liquid capital so that you can increase the velocity of your money and grow your wealth fast. But as you grow your wealth, if you want to truly have the Maui Lifestyle, then you will also have to transition some or all of your focus from investing for capital gains to investing for passive, residual income.

The key point is that forced appreciation takes time and energy to realize. It is the foundation of most great fortunes. But it should not be the stopping point.

Passive, Residual Cash Flow

We've already talked about the need to create passive cash flow if you want to be financially free, but now we need to drill down even deeper. You can make passive cash flow in the form of a lump sum payment you receive when you sell off an asset you own but didn't take more than 10 hours per month to oversee. But while this money may be passive, it still is just a one-time payment and not a secure income stream. Going back to our folk tale, it's a slaughtered goose and not the daily golden eggs. No matter how delicious that goose may be, it still won't feed you forever.

This is why Maui Millionaires know that they need to create not just passive cash flow, but more importantly, passive *residual* cash flow. Passive, residual cash flow is money that flows to you each month or quarter, year after year. It is out of passive, residual cash flow that true financial freedom is built.

So which is better, capital gains or residual cash flow? The answer is that you need both! Early on in your wealth building, you will be investing for what is called "forced appreciation." This is where you buy or build an asset and put in energy and work to vastly increase the value of that asset. For example, you might buy a foreclosure house for a 40 percent discount in price, fix it up, then resell it for a large profit. The house you paid $300,000 for was worth $500,000 when you sold it. This is an example of forced appreciation. You forced the asset to be $200,000 more valuable because you both fixed it up and you changed the circumstances of the person owning it. Now that you have created this equity, you might tap into it by selling (capital gain) and buying an even bigger property.*

Another example of forced appreciation comes when you grow a business. In the early years, you put in sweat equity to grow the market and your business's share of that market, knowing that if you are successful, you will be rewarded hundreds of times over for your time and effort. Many Maui Millionaires made their first fortune by starting and building a successful business of their own. For example, Stephanie and Jack, two Maui Millionaires from California, invested 17 years to build their thriving manufacturing business. Today that business is worth well over $15 million.

Once you reach a certain point you need to transition your wealth focus from forced appreciation to creating passive, residual cash flow. Let's look at this progression in detail.

Investment Focuses for Each of the Three Levels of Wealth Building

There are three distinct stages to your wealth building, each with specific, definite goals for you to focus on. For Level One wealth builders the essential focus is to learn enough to get started, with the biggest lesson being to learn to overcome your fear of getting started, so that you can get yourself into action. Level One is your departure point. It begins the moment you make the concrete decision to build great wealth. While in

---

*This is Diane, putting my CPA hat on for a moment. You can make this even better for yourself by taking advantage of specific tax loopholes like 1031 tax-free exchanges or investing with a tax-free Roth IRA LLC. For a FREE online workshop teaching you the top seven real estate investing tax loopholes go to **www.MauiMillionaireBook.com**.

The 3 Levels of Wealth Building

FREE

Level 3
Passive, Residual Cashflow!

FOCUS: Converting a large part of your net worth into secure income streams and solid, long-term investments.

LEVERAGE POINT: Invest for Cash flow

Level 2
Aggressive Growth

FOCUS: Building your asset base & financial skills.

LEVERAGE POINT: Invest for "Forced Appreciation"

Level 1
Getting Started!

FOCUS: Building a solid base of financial and investment skills.

LEVERAGE POINT: Invest in self via quality education and outside experts.

Level One, it's essential that you invest most heavily in your own financial education.

Practical education about wealth is critical in your development, and you will leverage this learning over a lifetime of wealth building. This learning can be from books, web sites, workshops, or mentors. It should also include focused debriefing of your actual wealth-building steps to suck as much learning from the marrow of your own experiences as possible. And it also should include leveraged learning by tapping into the expertise, outside perspective, and insights of your mastermind group.

During this stage of your wealth building, we recommend that you don't invest large amounts of money in any investment because you haven't developed the skills or network to give yourself the advantage you need to safely invest for the greatest returns. Instead, use the time and money to read the books, listen to the home study courses, and attend the financial and personal development workshops, so that you lay down a solid foundation upon which to build enduring wealth. A little bit of prudence and education will go a long way to helping you make intelligent financial choices in this early stage of your wealth building. How long will it take you to get through Level One?

Some Maui Millionaires blow through Level One in less than 90 days, while other Maui Millionaires take a year or two at this level to get up the courage to step up and into Level Two. We suggest you set the goal to take no more than 6 to 12 months at this level before you move into Level Two.

As a Level Two wealth builder it's time to begin building in earnest. It is in Level Two where you will have your steepest learning curve as a wealth builder. The focus of Level Two is to invest for aggressive equity growth. Now we want to make something very clear: Investing doesn't just mean investing in real estate, but it also means investing your energy in building or buying businesses. The key to Level Two is to invest not for appreciation but rather to only invest for *forced* appreciation. The difference is that investing for appreciation is the slow path to eventual wealth, while investing for forced appreciation is the route that all Maui Millionaires eventually find to build their fortune fast—in five years or less.

For example, you can buy a small apartment building, and over time that apartment building, if chosen correctly, will slowly go up in value as rents increase and the market matures in that area. This is one way to invest for ordinary appreciation. Forced appreciation would be to find an apartment building that you can buy below value, perhaps due to a high vacancy rate in the building. Then, once you buy the property, you actively and aggressively increase the occupancy rate and dramatically increase the value of the property. This active effort to change the circumstances of the building or of a business is how you as a wealth builder get the maximum equity growth that is the heart of forced appreciation.

David's Story

I remember one apartment complex I purchased where the vacancy factor was over 40 percent due to poor management. It took us about 12 months after we bought the complex to turn the property around to reduce the vacancy factor to 20 percent. At this point, we had already increased the value of the property by close to $2 million dollars just by filling up more of the units. This forced appreciation has been one of the biggest secrets to my wealth building over the years. In the beginning, it was what helped me buy houses from motivated sellers and resell those houses for $50,000 paydays. Later, it was what helped me grow my real estate training company from zero to a market value of millions. And it was also the secret that helped me teach several thousand students to make mega-millions as they bought and sold over $1 billion of real estate in a 10-year period.

The reason why it is so important for you to invest for forced appreciation in Level Two wealth building is because this is the fastest, surest road to wealth. For example, you may start a business with a few thousand dollars working out of your home—many Maui Millionaires have started with a whole lot less! You spend the next five years building and growing your business. At this point, it is generating hundreds of thousands of dollars of cash flow for you each year and has a market value many times what you started with. This is the beauty of forced appreciation—it allows you to leverage your time, talent, and energy to build wealth fast.

Now to get this forced appreciation in the early stages of your wealth building you are going to have to put in time and energy to create this value in the world. Later, you'll be able to harness other people through teams, systems, and outsourced solutions to unlock this powerful wealth-building potential.

As you start to aggressively grow your net worth, it's important to remember not to spend this equity on frivolous expenses. Why? Because this equity that you have so carefully and attentively grown is the seed capital for you to shift into the final wealth stage—Level Three. Level Three is where you have made the transition from active investing and business building to enjoying passive, residual cash flow. In Level Three, Maui Millionaires, who are all adept at converting cash and equity into passive, residual cash flow, transition a large portion of their net worth into hands-off income-generating investments. Ironically, it is from this place of total financial freedom that many Maui Millionaires take on their next business project that produces more forced appreciation than all their prior efforts combined. There is something that financial freedom adds to their wealth creations, almost like yeast to the baking of bread, that just makes the size, scope, and success of their projects go through the roof.

Level One is about starting the possibilities and going after forced appreciation, whether this be in building a business or buying an investment.

Level Two is about fine tuning your net worth building skills and active cash flow skills, and starting to make the shift to learn about creating passive, residual income.

Level Three is all about transitioning your wealth into passive, residual cash flows, whether this be by putting a business on autopilot, or by fine tuning your investment portfolio to churn out consistent, passive, residual income—year after year. When you are able to do this and generate enough income to pay for your lifestyle, then you will have become financially free and get to enjoy the real benefits of being a Maui Millionaire.

Wealth Factor Two: Net Worth

The second Wealth Factor is your Net Worth. This is the sum total of all your financial assets less any outstanding debts you owe. If cash flow is the key to pay for your day-to-day life, then your net worth is a key part of providing for your future security. In a short while, you are going to learn a breakthrough new way of looking at wealth that could literally double your net worth almost overnight.

But first, take a moment and determine what your current financial net worth is. Use the Maui Net Worth Worksheet to calculate it.

In the next section, we'll discuss wealth strategies that involve your cash flow. It's important to note the relationship between cash flow and value before we leave this section on assets.

Large properties, the type frequently bought by pension funds and

MAUI
Net Worth Worksheet

ASSETS

Cash on hand and in bank	$ _____
Savings Accounts	$ _____
IRA or Other Retirement Accounts...	$ _____
Life Insurance	$ _____
(cash surrender value only)	
Businesses	$ _____
(conservative equity if business is sold)	
Stocks & Bonds	$ _____
Real Estate	$ _____
Collectibles	$ _____
Other Assets	$ _____
Total Assets	$ _____

LIABILITIES

Accounts Payable	$ _____
Notes Payable to Banks & Others....	$ _____
Installment Accounts	$ _____
Monthly Payments	$ _____
Loan on Life Insurance	$ _____
Mortgages on Real Estate	$ _____
Unpaid Taxes	$ _____
Other Liabilities	$ _____
Total Liabilities	$ _____

Total Assets	$ _____
Less: Total Liabilities	$ _____
NET WORTH	$ _____

Take the Right Steps!!

insurance companies, are valued solely based on the cash flow. The relationship between the value of the property and the net operating income is called a capitalization rate. Let's say you have a property with an operating income of $100,000 per year. And, you're in an area where a 10 percent capitalization rate is common. The value of the property is $1,000,000. That's calculated as $100,000 divided by 10 percent.

Large properties, known as commercial properties, are often valued and compared as investment opportunities based on their capitalization rates. The higher the risk with a particular property, the higher the capitalization rate will need to be. In other words, more risk means the need for higher return.

There aren't as many clear-cut analysis points for value on businesses. In fact, there are many different ways, all approved and recognized by CPAs and other professionals, to value closely-held businesses. We prefer to look at the passive cash flow that comes from a business. When you sell products or services that are commoditized, you can create passive income from a business. The more passive income you receive, the more valuable your business is.

If you haven't already been convinced of the benefits of creating passive income from your business versus working hard and making earned income, here's one more reason. You'll make more money when you sell your business. If, and this is a big if, you are able to sell your business that you work in every day, you're usually lucky to get one times gross sales as a value. So, let's say you have a business that you work in and are able to bill $250,000 per year. That means the most you can generally hope to get is $250,000 if you can find a buyer.

Now, let's compare that to a sale of a business that is set up to provide passive income. First of all, by necessity, the business will have to be bigger. That's because it needs to provide the income to pay the salary of people that do the work for which you are paid, and for which you probably don't get paid such as administration and office work. Plus, your business also needs to provide the cash to pay you as an investor in the business.

So, rather than $250,000 in gross receipts, a passive company will generally have gross income jump by at least five times, which in our example would mean gross income of $1,250,000. Of course, that doesn't happen overnight, but that is generally the first milestone of a business. That means there will now be $1,250,000 in gross income, but rather than getting most of the income yourself, you'll have to first pay the expenses and salary for people who have replaced you.

Let's assume that leaves you 25 percent for the bottomline. In other words, you're making a little bit more than you did before—$312,500 instead of $250,000. But that $312,500 (25% of $1,250,000) is passive income and flows to you whether you work or not. Even better, as passive income it's taxed at a lower level. Despite all that, let's say you've made the decision to sell. This is where it gets really good.

Because it's a true passive business, you now have a lot of people interested in buying the company. You've opened it up for larger companies to buy and they typically pay five to eight times the net income for passive businesses. That means your company is now worth over $1,500,000.

Even if you don't want to sell, you can recognize the higher value on your personal balance sheet. So, your net worth has gone up because you've turned your earned income into passive income.*

Wealth Factor Three: Your R-Score

It's one thing to have a large net worth; it's quite another to be able to consistently convert that net worth into steady passive, residual income. Maui Millionaires have learned to master this key wealth skill, whether it be by investing in businesses or in real estate.

The amount of passive, residual income you are able to generate from your entire net worth is what determines your R-Score™. Your R-Score is your total return of passive, residual cash flow on your net worth. To calculate your R-Score you use the simple formula:

$$\text{R-Score} = \frac{\text{passive residual income(on an annual basis)}}{\text{net worth}}$$

For example, if you have a net worth of $500,000 and you have $25,000 of passive, residual income then your R-Score is 5 percent (25,000/$500,000).

Why Most People Are Measuring the Wrong Financial Indicator

It's the conventional wisdom that most wealth builders monitor their cash on cash return or COCR. But measuring COCR is deceptive because it is

---

*If you'd like to walk through the top five strategies for valuing a business, go to **www.MauiMillionaireBook.com**. You'll get to look over the shoulder of Diane as she puts her CPA hat on and values a business. You'll learn exactly how a financial expert evaluates a business and how you can increase the value of your business in leveraged ways so that when it's time to sell you double your profits!

too narrow a focus. You may have a net worth of $2 million and look at your $200,000 investment that is generating a 20 percent return (in other words, $40,000). This sounds great, but if your other $1.8 million is sitting idle then your true rate of return on the entire $2 million is actually just 2 percent. This is why we created your R-Score, because the Maui Millionaires needed a better economic measurement to assess their ability to convert net worth into cash flow, which is one of the seven key masterskills of the world's wealthiest people.*

Why is this so important? Because your R-Score is one of your most powerful leverage points to instantly increase your effective net worth. Let's examine this in closer detail.

How You Can Effectively Double Your Net Worth— Almost Overnight!

It is a mistake to think of your net worth only as a lump sum of money. Instead, Maui Millionaires know that your net worth is really the cash flow plant that produces cash flow. Don't just look at net worth as a asset, but think of it in terms of the passive residual cash flow you are able to generate from it. In fact, Maui Millionaires know that their effective net worth isn't fixed at any one moment. For example, take an ordinary millionaire with a net worth of $1 million. Imagine this millionaire had an R-Score of 5 percent. This means that each year the millionaire generates $50,000 from his $1 million net worth.

But what if you weren't just a millionaire, but instead you were a highly-skilled and financially-savvy Maui Millionaire with an R-Score of 10 percent? Assuming you had a net worth of that same $1 million your R-Score means that your net worth generates $100,000 a year of passive, residual income. You have *double* the cash flow from the same net worth. In a very real way when you double your R-Score you effectively *double* your net worth.

The real lesson here is clear. Your *effective* net worth is never fixed; it is directly correlated to your ability to invest it to generate a rate of return in the form of passive, residual cash flow. In other words, your R-Score multiplies the effective size of your net worth! This is why Maui Millionaires believe so strongly in the leverage of investing in their financial

---

*We have included an entire online workshop on the seven masterskills of the world's wealthiest people as part of your Maui Millionaire Wealth Mentorship Program. To get instant access to this valuable FREE bonus, just go to **www.MauiMillionaireBook.com**.

education. They've learned that each dollar wisely invested in their own earning capacity and financial fluency yields a hundredfold return in their effective net worth.

Think about it this way. If you could trade in your car that got 10 mpg for a car that got 20 mpg you would be able to go twice as far on the same amount of gas. This is the wealth-multiplying power of your R-Score.

Most people look at wealth one dimensionally—as a factor of their income (usually earned income at that!). But wealth has more dimensions than this. Wealth is also more than your net worth, which is the second dimension to your wealth. You need to add the third dimension into the picture to create financial depth. The third dimension of your financial wealth is your R-Score. (And just to keep your interest piqued, may we drop in an enticing teaser that in Chapter 19 we'll even share with you the *fourth* dimension of wealth that you've probably never read about in *any* financial book!)

Steve's Story

Steve was already a multimillionaire when he first came to Maui Mastermind. Yet his R-Score was very low. He hadn't transitioned from investing his net worth for capital gains to investing it to create passive, residual income. Over two years of attending Maui Mastermind, Steve learned how to leverage his wealth by investing in privately-held companies and real estate. As a result, his passive cash flow shot up over tenfold!

Steve not only increased his passive, residual cash flow by a factor of 10, but he also doubled his net worth. Since his net worth doubled, his R-Score was impacted. (Remember the R-Score is a factor of both of your cash flow and your net worth.) The bottom line is that even when he factored in his new net worth, by raising his R-Score so dramatically Steve effectively increased the cash-producing power of his net worth by an extra 500 percent!

Wealth Factor Four: The S-Factor

Being financially free means your passive residual income is more than enough to support your lifestyle. But how much does your current lifestyle cost? What does it cost you to live your life each year? Most people have no clue what their current lifestyle costs them on an annual basis. But if you don't know what it costs you to live your current lifestyle, how can you know how much passive, residual income you need to generate so that you can be financially free?

We term this number—the cost of your current lifestyle on an annual basis—your S-Factor™. As you can imagine, depending on what lifestyle you have chosen for yourself that number may be spartanly low or extravagantly high, or more likely somewhere in between. The simpler your tastes, the lower your S-Factor, which stands for *Simplicity Factor*. Are we suggesting that to become a Maui Millionaire you lead an ascetic life and disavow all desires for worldly possessions? Hardly. For now, we merely want you be aware of what your current S-Factor is so that you can make some intelligent choices about what is most important to you. We'll discuss this further in the next few pages.

But first, we want you to take a moment and estimate your current S-Factor. What do you think you currently spend to pay for your lifestyle each year? Or better yet, if you track your finances in a computer program like QuickBooks or Quicken, pull up what you spent over the last twelve months. Write that number in the box below.

We're about to share the Maui Financial Freedom Formula™ which focuses on the financial part of freedom, but before we do it is important to understand the nonfinancial aspect of your S-Factor—the cost in terms of time and energy you spend to maintain your current lifestyle.

All Maui Millionaires eventually come to realize that there are non-monetary costs to any lifestyle, and they learn to make the choices that are a fit for them as individuals. For example, both of us like beautiful houses, but David likes to go camping and rough it, while Diane appreciates the finer things in life like calling down for room service and getting a relaxing massage. Both are fantastic choices—for us. One thing every Maui Millionaire needs to figure out is what are the right choices—for you!

We recommend to all wealth builders that you simplify your life so that it has fewer moving parts to it. We suggest you cut back or hire other people to handle the daily upkeep on your lifestyle wherever you can. For example, hire someone to clean your house and maintain your lawn. Simplify your financial house so your bills are paid automatically via a credit card whose bill in turn is automatically paid from a checking account you have set up to pay bills from. The idea is to eliminate or outsource the things you personally have to do on a day-to-day or month-by-month basis so that you can instead spend that time where you most want to. This is a key part of creating a Maui Lifestyle.

Okay, it's time to tie this all together with a simple formula to become financially free.

The Maui Financial Freedom Formula

Let's spend some time talking about what financial wealth really is. Most people measure financial wealth in dollars—in terms of net worth. But this is misleading. A more accurate measure of wealth in the context of becoming financially free is time. How long can your money keep you in your current lifestyle without your having to actively work?

The way you win the money game is when the income your net worth generates is greater than your cost of living. This is what everyone's first financial freedom goal should be—to have the cash flow your assets generate pay for your lifestyle. Then from this base of freedom you can supersize your dreams and grow your wealth to have more options available to yourself.

Here is the fancy, "official" version of the Maui Financial Freedom Formula.

Maui Financial Freedom Formula

Passive Residual Income (PRI) / S-Factor

If that number is greater than one, you are financially free.
If it is less than one, you still have a ways to go.

Diane's Story

Since I'm a CPA at heart, I like it when the formulas come out. When you look at your Maui Financial Freedom Score™, you might have noticed that there are actually three different points you control: R-Score, S-Factor, and your net worth. A change in any one of these can improve your Maui Financial Freedom Score.

One of my lifestyle strategies is that whenever I increase my S-Factor, it has to be offset by a change in either my R-Score or net worth that is double the S-Factor change.

As an example, I really wanted a Series 6 BMW convertible. I knew the best way for tax purposes to buy something like that was to actually lease it through my business and take the deduction for the business portion of the car. So, my rule was that, although it was a business expense, I still had to create another $3,000 per month in passive residual income to cover the $1,500 increase in my S-Factor. The reason I always go higher is in case there is some unforeseen circumstance that makes the PRI drop for a particular month. I never want my S-Factor items to put my sense of well being at risk. In this case, I also needed to find a way for my partner to get the same benefit. That meant we needed an additional $6,000 per month in passive income.

We'd had a plan on the drawing board for awhile that needed just a little bit of work to create more passive income for our company. Neither one of us had been too motivated to do it yet. Now, we had the motivation! We increased the R-Score for our business to make it happen.

I had my new car within a month.

How far do you have to go before you are financially free? That depends on two things. It depends on your passive, residual cash flow and it depends on your S-Factor.

Your passive residual cash flow is the result of two things: your net worth and your R-Score. For example, let's say you have a net worth of $200,000 and an R-Score of 5 percent. This generates a PRI (Passive Residual Income) of $10,000 per year. If you increase your R-Score from 5 percent to 10 percent you have just effectively doubled your PRI from $10,000 to

$20,000. You can also achieve the same result by doing a business or investment deal that moves your net worth from $200,000 to $400,000. With your original R-Score of 5 percent this will generate $20,000 per year of PRI.

You can use this understanding to work backward to your goal. Let's say your goal is to generate $10,000 per month of PRI ($120,000 per year). If your current R-Score is 10 percent, then you can quickly calculate that you'll need a net worth of $1,200,000 to reach your PRI goal. (PRI = NW × R-Score) (NW = PRI/R-Score) (R-Score = PRI/NW) $120,000/10 percent = $1,200,000 net worth needed.

Another way to accelerate your way to financial freedom is to lower your S-Factor. If you can reduce your current S-factor of $120,000 per year to $80,000 per year you've just made it 33 percent easier to reach your goal of financial freedom.

Here's the real key. Balance your desire for financial freedom with your current enjoyment of life, *but* remember our recommendation is to get yourself financially free as fast as possible. This is best achieved by lowering your S-Factor, growing your net worth, and increasing your R-Score in combination. Then from this place of first-order financial freedom, build and create the wealth to reach higher-order financial freedom goals. Maui Millionaires understand that once they get financially free it becomes easier and easier, and faster and faster, to move to ever-increasing amounts of financial prosperity and abundance.

Jeff's Story

It's said that the second million is always easier and that's been proven true by Maui Millionaires such as Jeff who learned how to look at properties with his new W.O.S.

When Jeff first came to Maui that first year, he was a brand new millionaire. It had taken him a lot of time and effort to earn that first million, and he had a blast sharing his story with his fellow wealth builders in Maui. But it was after his second Maui that he kicked his wealth building into overdrive and started making well over a half million per project. For example, one project that took a $250,000 down payment (which he got back in option payments within seven months) ended up putting $625,000 total profit in his pocket from the project. The next one gave him a cash return of 15 percent plus another $600,000 of cash profits when he sells the property later this year.

You don't have to have money to make money, but it does make it a lot easier.

Wealthy people know that in the beginning they trade off short-term, instant gratification for real, enduring financial freedom, which ultimately is worlds more gratifying then the fleeting fix of feeding a momentary urge.

Where do wealthy people sacrifice in the beginning and middle stages of their wealth building? In the dressings of wealth, in the façade of wealth. It's often not the wealthy who drive the fancy cars and eat in the expensive restaurants, it's the middle class. And do you know how they pay for it? By mortgaging their future to fill their urges today. For example, the average American by age 50 has a net worth of less than zero. They owe more than they own.

This is insanity! Maui Millionaires know that by letting go in the beginning of much of this ego-driven "stuff," that in the end they will have it all! They will have the financial ability to buy what they want to buy and to have the freedom to enjoy it.

Here's the payoff, while most people spend 40-plus years readying themselves for retirement, and still over 95 percent of them fail, remaining dependent on the government or family for the main source of their income, Maui Millionaires reach financial freedom in a fraction of that time. In fact, most Maui Millionaires take less than five years to earn their financial freedom, once they have their first Maui Awakening. So we want to be clear here. We are not advocating living on limited means and dampening all your dreams and desires to live a fabulous lifestyle. We are saying instead, that by consciously choosing to redirect your earnings to go back into your wealth creation for a short while, within five years you can become financially free. It's when you reach this first order of financial freedom that you'll be able to see a whole new world of riches and opportunities. In the end, this will help you build more wealth, faster, because you will be starting from a much more powerful place of being.

Kelly and Rob's Story

Kelly and Rob went from credit card debt of $77,000 to Maui Millionaires in just two years. Kelly used an even tougher definition of being a millionaire. She insisted on having a million dollars of net worth not counting their personal residence. And, most amazing of all, the only way they found to achieve that was by both of them quitting their jobs!

Now there are two places that Maui Millionaires are willing to invest heavily during the early and middle stages of their wealth building, and this investing continues throughout their lives.

First, they invest heavily in themselves. Maui Millionaires all know that the fastest path to wealth is through consistently investing in both their personal development and in growing their earning capacity. Maui Millionaires take the classes, they read the books, and they listen to the home study courses. In addition, they cultivate relationships with experienced mentors who can help advise and guide them on their journey.* They also build a network of other positive and growing wealth builders with whom they can mastermind, bounce ideas off, and share key contacts. Remember, you are the container for your wealth. The more you grow, the more your wealth can grow.

The second place where Maui Millionaires are willing to invest heavily during the early and middle stages of their wealth building, and this investing continues throughout their lives, is in their giving. Maui Millionaires consistently share a percentage of their time, their talent, and their money helping others in charitable activities. In fact, we are about to say something that is going to shock many readers. We believe it is impossible to be truly wealthy without being extremely generous with your time, talent, and money in helping the world.

Wealth Factor Five: Peace of Mind

With all this focus on the financial elements of wealth, it is imperative that we take a moment to get clear on the *human* elements of wealth. Remember, it isn't enough to have just the money, Maui Millionaires have money plus. They have money plus the time to enjoy it. They have money plus the relationships to share it. They have money plus the sense of purpose and passion with which to direct it. And they have money plus the connection to a higher power or deeper meaning to ground it.

It is our hope that you set your sights higher than merely becoming a

---

*To download a list of David's "Top 10 Power Questions to Ask Your Mentors," just go to **www.MauiMillionaireBook.com**. Plus, would you like to hear Diane and David's answers to these same ten questions? There is a special audio interview with each of them as they share their surprising answers to these direct and powerful questions. Just go to **www.MauiMillionaireBook.com** to listen to both these interviews absolutely FREE.

millionaire. Instead, we want you to become a Maui Millionaire. When you have all the money that you'll ever need, what is your life going to be about that gives it meaning above and beyond the money? Remember, the money is just a power source to amplify your ability to live your life's real purpose. What is your vision for your life? What are the values you will strive to live in accordance with? It's this focus on living consistent with your vision and values that leads to the integral life of a Maui Millionaire.*

Diane's Story

My husband and I made a lot of changes in our life when we made the decision to adopt David. I don't know if we could have made those changes if we hadn't had the freedom that comes from being Maui Millionaires who have complete financial freedom.

David is now 15. He has gone up six grade levels in English comprehension in less than a year and is a competitive figure skater with dozens of friends. If he were still in Mexico, he'd most likely be working in a factory at $1.00 per hour, if he had survived.

One day he turned to me when we were driving to a doctor's office and said, "I knew it would be good to have a family, but I never expected you to love me so much."

The time we are able to spend with David is a demonstration of the love we feel. None of this would have been possible without the financial freedom to consciously and purposely choose the course of our life. That's what being a Maui Millionaire means to me.

---

*Would you like to participate in a powerful online Vision and Values Workshop? Just go to **www.MauiMillionaireBook.com**. and click on the "Online Workshops" tab.

CHAPTER 18

The Maui Wealth Scorecard—How to Know Your *Real* Score in the Financial Freedom Game

Far too many people will never create financial freedom for themselves simply because they unwittingly fool themselves as to the real status and direction of their financial lives. Maui Millionaires know that in order to win the financial freedom game they need to consistently be updated with a meaningful measure of financial score and trend points. When you have this information, in a reliable, consistent, and simplified format, you are able to make accurate financial decisions and accelerate your progress toward financial freedom.

Wealth Trap

Fooling yourself as to the real score of the game.

People fool themselves about the real status of their finances for three primary reasons.

First, far too many people simply take the path of least resistance and do nothing. They put their long-term financial future into the hands of other people because it's both easy and the expected thing to do. Never mind that this is an almost certain path to financial failure! Yes, it takes energy and effort to put your financial house in order and become financially free. But it takes a hundred times more energy and effort over the long haul to live a life financially strapped and dependent on outside agencies for your mere survival. The old saying is still true: An ounce of prevention is worth a pound of cure.

The second reason people fool themselves about their current financial status is ignorance. Many people have never learned the financial skills nor had the financial education to understand where they actually stand financially. But remember, you are totally responsible for your financial success, and ignorance is not an excuse, it's merely a cop out and acceptance of financial failure. With just the simple skills you've picked up in this book, you have the knowledge you need to take charge of your financial destiny.

The final reason so many people fool themselves over the real condition of their financial life is fear and shame. Countless millions of people are afraid to even look at their financial status because it's just too scary for them or filled with painful feelings of shame. For example, they may have lived well beyond their means and as a result lost ground every year. The idea of anyone—themselves, their spouse, or any outside person—finding out about their true financial situation is too scary and threatening to them. So what do they do? They rationalize, they fantasize, they obscure, they ignore, they distract, or they flat out deny the truth. That is until their financial house of cards comes crashing down.

So what's the solution to this challenge? First, it is to understand that the foundation of all wealth is a solid W.O.S. This means begin today the process of upgrading your W.O.S. to empower you to get richer results. With this understanding, it becomes a lot less scary to look at the real score of your financial game accurately and objectively. This is where the Maui Wealth Scorecard™ comes into play.

Begin today to direct a specific percentage of your time and income to invest in your real wealth. Your goal is to reach the wealth producing place of 20-plus percent of your income and time going into wealth-producing activities that directly enrich you. Let's be clear, this is not you working a second job. This is you investing in assets, whether it's a business or a property that you can help significantly go up in value. Later, once you have a large net worth, you can shift your wealth into easier passive wealth producers. But early on you can accelerate your wealth building by putting in some leveraged time. Is this different from how the average worker diverts a little money out of her paycheck into her company 401k or pension fund, then waits 40-plus years to retire? You bet it is. You can take the slow, steady, gradual path to retirement. There is nothing wrong with this choice, except that it takes a disciplined effort over 40 years or longer to achieve. Plus at the end, it leads only to a "comfortable" retirement, not a retirement of freedom and passion.

The Three Wealth Accelerators

As the final section to this part of the book, we'd like to share with you three powerful Wealth Accelerators™ that you can use to become financially free faster and easier.

Wealth Accelerator One: Leverage

Leverage is when a unit of effort produces a magnified result. In wealth building, the greatest key to success is working smarter not harder, and this means leverage. It's what allows Maui Millionaires to consistently generate large and growing monthly cash flows while working fewer and fewer hours. There are two main forms of leverage.

First is what we call personal leverage. This is when you leverage your own personal efforts, finances, and contacts to get better and bigger results. This form of leverage includes consistently choosing the highest payoff activities while focused on your wealth building and letting go of the lower-level work, or intelligently leveraging your money in your business building, such as when you invest it in your marketing efforts.

Personal leverage also includes the power of your relationship skills and health promotion efforts. Never forget that some of the most expensive wealth land mines, not to mention painful experiences to go through, are broken relationships, be they a messy divorce or an ugly business partnership shakedown. And think how much excellent health adds to your quality of life and ability to create more wealth. The investments you make in improving your relationship skills and caring for your health produce long-term, magnified returns for you. They are a core part of personal leverage.

Next there is "external leverage." External leverage comes when you leverage outside forces to accelerate your wealth building. This could be through tapping into the power of other people's time, contacts, ideas, money, and expertise. For example, a personal assistant allows you to leverage his time to get better results in your wealth building. Or you could use outside financing to fund a business or investment deal that is too large for you to do on your own. Or perhaps you could get a key idea

Maui
WEALTH Scorecard

○ WEALTH Scorecard.
  2 key Indicators
  • R-Score = Passive Income on PR Cash flow.
              Net Worth.
  • S-Factor. = Cost of Living
              All the money you spend in a Year.

Part One: Your R-Score

R-Score = Passive, Residual income over past 12 months

÷

Net Worth

	Current	Last Check-in	% Change
PRI			
Net Worth			
R-Score			

Part Two: Your S-Factor

S-Factor = $ spent on living for past 12 months

Peace of Mind Score: 1 – 10

	Current	Last Check-in	% Change
S-Factor			
Peace of Mind			

MAUI FINANCIAL FREEDOM SCORE

$$\frac{Total\ Passive + Passive\ Residual}{S\text{-}Factor}$$

- If the number is greater than $1 \longrightarrow$ you are free!
  If the number is less than $1 -$ you are not.

FREE

	Current	Last Check-in	% Change
PRI			
S-Factor			
Maui Financial Freedom Score			

1st Stage Financial Freedom Goal (Should be at least your S-Factor):   By: _____

2nd Stage Financial Freedom Goal   By: _____

Ultimate Financial Freedom Goal   By: _____

What three to five things are you most pleased about in this area of your life?

What one or two things will you do differently over the next 90 days that will give you the greatest return or have the most significant, positive impact on this area of your life?

What are three specific action steps you will take in the next 30 days to implement these changes or improvements?

Go to **www.MauiMillionaireBook.com** and not only download a copy of this powerful wealth scorecard, but participate in a free online workshop that walks you step-by-step through exactly how to use this wealth tool to accelerate your way to financial freedom! For full details see the Appendix.

from an outside mentor who saves you months of figuring out a key process all on your own. External leverage helps Maui Millionaires reach their financial goals many times faster than most ordinary millionaires.

Wealth Accelerator Two: Clarity

Clarity comes when you have a concrete vision of what it is that you want to accomplish and the values and standards that guide your efforts to create that outcome. We've both watched many ordinary millionaires end up empty because they focused on the wrong end. They mistakenly thought that if they had money then they would be happy. But Maui Millionaires know that the truth is that you are happy when you happily build your wealth. Happiness is a skill and attitude that must be practiced along the way.

Truly, there is power when you take the time to accurately identify what matters most to you and keep that clearly in mind as you build your wealth. There is no greater waste than to spend a lifetime building a dream that doesn't matter to you.

When we sat down to build the Maui Millionaire, LLC, we first focused on what was the real driving force behind our wanting to build this business. We both were at the place financially where we didn't need the money, so that wasn't what was driving us forward. We went through a proprietary process that helped us discover the passion that drove us both. We were starting and growing the business to bring the humanity back into wealth building. We both felt to the core of our beings that for too long people had gone about their wealth building in a values vacuum. We wanted to teach generations of wealth builders the power, joy, and freedom of building wealth Maui-style—in all areas of their life. And we also wanted to help them understand that it's not a responsibility of the wealthy to give, it's not just a requirement, but rather it's a joy to give and share your wealth with the world.

We went on to clarify five dominant values that we agreed we would build into the very DNA of our business so that we always remember exactly why we began this business in the first place.* What are the driv-

---

*Would you like to learn what we chose as our five dominate values for the Maui Millionaires business and how you can use this same powerful model in your own wealth building? Then log onto **www.MauiMillionaireBook.com** and click on the "Our Mission" tab.

ing forces behind your business? What are the values to which you will hold true? What are the standards you will live your life in accordance with? When you are clear on these things, all your efforts take on a cleaner, sharper, more focused edge.

Wealth Accelerator Three: Community

You've already learned how your W.O.S. is so critical in your wealth building. But remember, the community you identify yourself with is one of the strongest factors in how your W.O.S. is fashioned. Maui Millionaires understand that their community of peers is what makes building real wealth so much easier and faster for them. That is why they spend so much time and effort to consciously create a community of positive, generous, like-minded individuals to mutually support each other in the pursuit of wealth and living a life that matters.*

In summary, in this part of the book you have learned about the five Wealth Factors—Cash Flow, Net Worth, R-Score, S-Factor, and Peace of Mind. You have also learned about what it means to build Level Three Wealth. And, finally, you have learned a simple, yet powerful, scorekeeping system to track your wealth-building results so you always know where you stand.

In the next part, you'll learn about the power of Maui Giving, and why it is literally impossible to become wealthy without fully embracing this philosophy of abundance.

---

*To immediately tap into the Maui wealth-building community, go to **www.MauiMillionaireBook.com** right away!

PART FIVE

MAUI WEALTH LEVERAGE STRATEGY FIVE:
Tap into Maui Giving to Create a Legacy That Lives On Beyond You!

CHAPTER 19

Real Wealth
Is What You Give

What are your beliefs about giving? Many of us have a mixed bag of old programs about money and giving. You might have been taught that it is better to give then it is to receive. And yet, at the same time, you might have been taught that the way to wealth and security is to hang on to money. Be frugal above all other things. And your religious training might have included the idea that money is the root of all evil. All of these are powerful beliefs about money and impact how wealthy you eventually become.

As you processed through the five steps to upgrade your Wealth Operating System, you learned how your beliefs shape your financial destiny. Now we want to let you in on a little-known secret: Maui Giving is one of the most powerful ways you can effortlessly upgrade your Wealth Operating System! Giving might be the quickest way to get massive results in how you view wealth.

Consider what happens when you contribute money. One of the quickest ways to lose your detachment to the feeling that money is scarce is to give it away. In fact, it's the greatest affirmation about your future wealth-making ability. If you knew you could easily make money and lived and acted with that confidence, then it wouldn't be necessary for you to horde your money. If money flowed to you easily, all you would need to do is just grab another bucket and fill it with the available abundance. Now, don't worry too much here. We are not advocating giving everything away and waiting around to receive more. No, in fact, it's often necessary to have money as a seed for the next big project.

Instead, we are talking about powerful, outside-of-the-box giving that actually makes you wealthier. You stretch beyond where you are currently and act with faith that you will receive more.

Throughout this chapter, we'll talk about some of the lessons that Maui Millionaires have learned about giving and how important it is to their personal wealth building. It's important to remember that not only can you contribute your money, but it's equally important and valuable for you to contribute your time and talent too. It's commonly taught that it's important to tithe or contribute 10 percent of your money. But, have you ever considered also tithing your time and talent? Yes, it is important to write those checks, but by sharing your time and talent you are able to increase the impact of your giving and emotionally connect to the giving you are involved with in a deeply-satisfying way.

Here are five reasons that Maui Millionaires state for why they give.

It's the Right Thing to Do

You'll feel good. If you're feeling a little down, depressed, or simply at your wit's end, give. The human connection never ceases to amaze in how quickly it will restore spirits.

We want to be very clear here. We are not advocating that the reason to help people is to feel good about yourself because you are somehow better than they are. Instead, it's a feeling of doing good that makes you feel good. The best thing a teacher can do is teach so well that a pupil exceeds the accomplishments of the teacher. That's the kind of giving that a Maui Millionaire believes in.

One of the projects that Maui Millionaires, LLC, has adopted is a five-year funding commitment for the Justa Center, a shelter for homeless families in Phoenix. Prior to the Justa Center, families were not allowed at the only other center—the Homeless Resource Center—located in downtown Phoenix, because registered sex offenders were paroled to that facility. Families were not allowed to be near the registered sex offenders, which made sense. But what didn't make sense was that the over 4,000 homeless children in Phoenix had no place to shower, get medical or dental care, or just have a chance to safely play for a little bit while their moms and dads accessed social services to help them transition off the streets.

When we saw the reality of what homeless families were facing, and the lack of resources to help them get off the streets and back into mainstream society, we knew we had to do it. There was no question. Our hearts simply told us it was the right thing to do. It required that we stretch ourselves because it was something none of us had ever done before. And, of course, once stretched, you can never go back to the way you were before. Can you think of a better way to push yourself to grow?

Abundance Thinking

It's one thing to drop a dollar or two in the collection plate at church every Sunday. It's a completely different thing to set a goal of paying for all school fees for every orphan at the 227 orphanages in Juarez, Mexico, or to reduce the rate of recidivism for prisoners by teaching them powerful life-coping skills. Those are the type of projects that make you gasp just a little bit. And, when you do that, you expand what you know you can do. Those are both projects taken on by Maui Masterminders as part of the Maui Mastermind event.

Beverly Sallee, one of the Maui Mastermind Stars, tells the story that changed her view of giving. It happened at her church one Sunday. The pastor brought a cute little boy up front with him. He showed the boy two cookies and then proceeded to eat one. He raved about how good the cookie tasted and how it just melted in his mouth. The poor boy could hardly contain himself waiting for the pastor to hand him his own cookie. Imagine how he felt when the pastor instead said, "You know, I might need this one later. I think I should just keep it."

That's the same thing that we do when we hang onto something (just in case), when others need the same resource. We might withhold money from needy causes or time from our family—hoarding it "in case" we need it later.

Remember, Maui Giving is the greatest affirmation of your abundance and prosperity that you can make. It's you making a powerful declaration that you have more than enough—more than enough time, more than enough talent, and more than enough money.

Again and again, we hear people say things like "money changes people" or, "he's rich—you know what that means." Wealth is attributed to having some deep profound change on people's personalities turning a wonderful human being into Scrooge.

A hallmark of determining whether someone is going to be a Maui Millionaire is to see what happens when she gets money. Sometimes the money is inherited and very rarely, those beneficiaries have been taught about their social and financial responsibilities with money. On his wedding day, Bill Gates, co-founder of Microsoft, received a card from his mother that said, "With great wealth comes great responsibilities." He says that moment changed his life, and he and his wife vowed to devote massive amounts of money and time to charitable giving. Unfortunately, many rich kids have never been taught the responsibility of their position and use it instead as a ticket to party like no one else.

It's not a lot different, though, from the people that suddenly get a flush of cash due to an outstanding athletic talent, sudden inheritance, or winning lottery ticket. To modify an old saying, "a fool and his money is one big party!" And, boy, is that the case sometimes.

Still others build wealth and treat it as a fluke. They never invest or build a business again. They become stingy, hanging on to every penny, uncertain how long this undeserved windfall can possibly last before someone figures out they never should have had the money to begin with.

Then, there are those amazing people—the Maui Millionaires—who use wealth as a leverage point to empower themselves, their family, and their communities to create even more. They are driving to continue building their wealth because they have more riding on it. It's also a whole lot of fun.

The difference between the Maui Millionaires and everyone else is that they truly believe in abundance and that they deserve what they have. They don't have the need to self-destruct their lives or search for ever more external gratification. They keep the dreams of their heart close to them. They find great joy in leveraged giving.

Money doesn't change people, it reveals character.

If you want to give more, you're going to have to have more. You will push yourself to bigger deals and a larger acceptance of wealth in your lifetime. Why not set a goal of being a Carnegie or Rockefeller, dedicating millions to the good of humanity?

If you want to push yourself to have more, then we suggest you connect that with pushing yourself to give more.

Kathleen came to Maui Mastermind originally to learn how to take her already successful business up not just one notch, but five notches. She discovered that Maui touched her life in an unexpected way. Here's Kathleen's story, in her own words.

Estrellas Para Ninos (Stars for Children)

I'm currently the Communication Director of Estrellas Para Ninos. It's a nonprofit that started out of Maui, set up to aid orphanages in Cuidad Juarez, Mexico. This past year, I saw our group jump from 6 people to 29 people. I thought, *We really did something here. One person can make a difference.*

I think what happens if you just get it started is that other people will see the value and get inspired. It just takes getting it started.

(continued)

Estrellas Para Ninos (Stars for Children) *(continued)*

I felt very blessed in my life and I've wanted to find a way to do something to give back for a long time. Maui was the right place to make it happen.

Now that I've been involved with Estrellas Para Ninos in Juarez, I find that the things that I would normally get worried about just aren't that important. When you spend time with children who truly have nothing, you look at your life differently. You live life abundantly and with fullness because everything is more precious. I was able to share just a little that I was blessed with.

Abundance in giving means abundance in my business as well. Recently, I was telling some others about my properties in New York. I have a field partner who handles a lot of the on-site management issues. Someone came up to me and asked for the name of my field partner. For a minute, I thought about not giving out her name. I was worried about sharing a resource and creating my own competition.

But then I remembered the example of empowering the children in Juarez. We found that there is an abundance of wealth, opportunities, deals, and money. You only really understand and demonstrate that abundance when you can give it away. That might mean writing a check to a charity or sharing a resource.

My three words for making a giving project work are inspiration, organization, and persistence. Someone needs to keep the communication working. Be patient with others. It's part of my belief in my faith that it's important to let people come into the project in their own way without judgment. I view wealth the same way now. Money is just one little piece of true wealth.

Kathleen's work with Estrellas Para Ninos is inspirational.* She has three tips for making a project work.

1. Set aside profit from specific business or investment deals for charitable contribution.
2. Talk about the project with everyone.
3. If you don't ask, you don't get.

The More You Earn, the More You Have to Share

It could be that you're struggling with the concept that there is nothing wrong with having or wanting money. Maybe it sometimes feels a little greedy and uncomfortable to want more. If you struggle with those feelings, consider giving more. Here's why.

When you see yourself using your wealth to bless other people's lives, it gives you tacit permission to generate great wealth. You become a steward using your wealth in healthy, responsible, and generous ways. It's a way of keeping you in the game, if you see the reality that making money really is a game. You don't have to be limited simply because there isn't anything else materially you want. When you take on a cause that is bigger than you are, you are forced to grow. And making money is not only okay, it becomes divine purpose.

This is especially true if you can invest and build businesses in a way that elevates others as well. For some people, making money looks like a zero sum game. In other words, if you make money, someone else loses money. That type of viewpoint assumes that there are limited resources and limited rewards in our world. It's why wars are fought, and why businesses battle. They feel there is only so much of the prize available and the only way to receive is to take it from someone else.

Actually, if you look at making money that way, it makes a lot of sense why there are so many religious and humanitarian concerns about having

---

*Would you like to get a behind-the-scenes look at some exclusive video footage of the charity work that Estrellas Para Ninos and other Maui Millionaires are doing to help the world? Just go to **www.MauiMillionaireBook.com** and click on the "Maui Giving" tab. You'll learn lots of ideas about how you and your organizations can use the lessons from other Maui Millionaires to leverage your giving to create a legacy that lives beyond your lifetime. For complete details see the Appendix.

wealth. If you believe in scarcity, then you've had to take from someone else to find wealth. There is an implication that you have to have hurt someone else to have anything in this world. Based on that belief, it would certainly be more in keeping with the concept of universal or divine love to share equally.

But, what if there is another way? What if it is possible to combine one or more products with the magic of innovation to create something that is bigger than the sum of the parts? It's the case of 1 plus 1 = 11, not 2. No, this isn't just bad math, it's something that's called synergy, and it's an integral part of being a Maui Millionaire.

What if you could take a business idea and supersize it so that your customers and vendors alike were educated and prospered as a result of doing business with you? Now, take that same idea and educate your employees so that they become financially independent. Sure, you might lose them when they don't need to work for you anymore because they have the means to support themselves. But think about another viewpoint. Imagine a business where the people working for you worked there because they were passionate about your business mission and goals. They didn't need the money and didn't struggle with day-to-day financial and living issues. They had true wealth in their lives. They came to work everyday energized and excited about what they could create in the fertile playground you had provided.

When you change your viewpoint about making money, and educate and empower others around you with the same ideals, you can change the realities for a lot of people.

Raises the Bar on the Game

It's said that a rut is just a grave with the ends kicked out. Living as human beings, we have a tendency to settle into our comfort zone of yesterday and stop growing and stretching. When you commit to Maui Giving, it's your chance to raise the bar on how you play the game of life. And with your increased expectations comes greater growth and learning.

Opens Doors

When you add in the component of giving, suddenly doors open that normally wouldn't be open. Remember when we talked about the synergy of dreams that occurs when you combine your dreams with someone else's? The same thing happens when you combine giving with your business plans.

The way you get your dreams, or your deal, is that you are now helping someone else get her dream. It's a way to overcome barriers. The differences in status simply go away. It's a way of saying that every person has value and there is a need to respect him. And, after all, isn't that why commerce exists? It's a way to provide a system of equitable and efficient delivery of products and services. At the purest level of freedom of trade, barriers come down, and everyone benefits to the extent of the perceived value of their contribution. Unfortunately, capitalism is a two-edged sword. The other side of pure capitalism is its cold economic efficiency. If people don't have value, in a way recognized by an economy, they don't receive the benefits of that economy. And that leaves children huddling in rags on the street corner and people pushed beyond the bounds of human tolerance.

Now suddenly, whether homeless or a king, all will benefit when you combine the efficiencies of a successful business with heart.

Beverly's Story

We often say, "Don't talk about me when I am gone."

Usually the saying is meant in jest. But, often, kidding has a point. Many people *are* afraid of what others might say about them when they're gone.

Have you ever thought about reversing that fear? What could it mean to ensure that people will talk about you when you're gone? You can do that through conscious decisions you make throughout your lifetime. What will people say about you when you're gone?

Consider some powerful people who have lived before us. In the case of Howard Hughes, most would say he was very wealthy and a smart, innovative guy. However, his life ended tragically. Now, we remember him as a loner and complete eccentric. In the case of Andrew Carnegie, most would remember him as a wealthy, smart, and innovative financial leader of his day. Now, after he's gone, we mostly remember all the good he did for society as he dedicated the final decades of his life to working to healthfully give away his huge fortune to bless humanity. His humanitarian efforts overshadowed his business accomplishments.

In my case, I clearly remember the day it dawned on me that the old adage is true: "The bed can only be so soft." I decided the rest of my life would be spent building significance. That would be the result of my continued success.

(continued)

Beverly's Story *(continued)*

As my schooling and early profession were in the music field, I began to give scholarships to worthy students in underdeveloped countries. Later, I deliberately opened markets in third world countries in order to help local charitable efforts.

I'm still amazed at how business can grow when the word gets around that you are donating to charity!

I now have 50 foreign affiliate companies. Each and every one of them has some type of charitable organization or benefit tied to them. In fact, I won't start a new affiliate *unless* there is a way to give back to the local community through the proceeds.

So, I hope they *do* talk about me when I'm gone. But I don't want it to be because of what I earned or what I had, but instead, because of what I gave away.

Giving is a fundamental part of a Maui business. There's a feeling of "it's what we should do," but it's actually more because the giving itself transforms how you view wealth and how you view yourself in the world. It's not just because it's the right thing to do, or even because of how it sparks you to grow. Rather it's because Maui Millionaires have learned that true giving has become one of their greatest joys and dominant inspirations and passions in life. It's allowed them to move from success to significance.

CHAPTER 20

Using Leverage to Sustain Giving Beyond Your Lifetime

A tragedy strikes. There is a rush of attention from the media. Sympathy is high, and the money rolls in. Then, slowly, no matter how horrific the tsunami, hurricane, earthquake, or terrorist attack, the attention fades. The media all go home. The money stops. But that doesn't mean the problems have been solved. They've just, sadly, been superceded by the latest more popular need.

One of the hallmarks of the wealthiest is that they set up a legacy of giving that lasts beyond their lifetime. Alfred Nobel invented dynamite and was mortified when he saw this wondrous invention used in war. He decided to devote his money and energy into rewarding people who brought goodness into the world. That was the beginning of the Nobel Prizes for physics, chemistry, medicine, literature, and peace.

The legacies of the Rockefellers, the Kennedys, Carnegie, Gates, and numerous others are the memories of wealthy people who looked beyond their own lifetime and what they personally could do. They created something that was bigger than anything they could hope for in that lifetime. They created sustained giving.

If you want to have true wealth in the most complete way possible, with a sense of purpose, happiness, and joy that goes beyond—and want to fully experience the confidence and peace that comes from giving—give like the rich do. Use leverage to sustain giving beyond your lifetime.

Leverage Your Business

Sustained giving can be achieved by businesses that go on beyond you, enrich other people, and instill them with the fire of giving

If you have a business that has giving as a significant part of its purpose, you will find that the idea catches fire within the business. Employees, vendors, and customers alike pick up the spirit and carry it on.

Maui Millionaire Morgan Smith was so inspired about the concept of Maui Giving after the first year's Maui Mastermind event that he put into place a companywide program whereby his employees can volunteer to have a specific amount of their pretax income set aside for charity. This money is gathered together, and the employees decide on which causes or charities to donate the money to. Last year, for example, they gave a large part of it to help the victims of the Gulf Coast hurricanes, and also to build a water filtration plant to give clean, safe drinking water to an entire village in Africa.

Morgan shared how once upon a time, at their annual company dinner, he would talk about how the company had made such and such a profit, and hit other financial markers. Now, at their annual company dinners he talks about how the company has raised thousands of dollars for great causes and touched so many lives. It has totally transformed the feelings of those people who are part of Morgan Financial.

From a business perspective, aside from the moral considerations, which company would you rather work for? An ordinary company that is focused just on the bottom line, or a Maui business that has a deep commitment to tie its business in with charitable works? Which style of company would you rather own? We know Morgan has made the right decision and believe that any business could implement this powerful idea and generate a huge competitive advantage.

Here are three strategies to create sustained giving with your business.

Have a Business That Funds Giving

An easy way to create giving as a fundamental part of your business is to set aside a percentage of your profit right from the beginning. As your business grows, your giving grows.

Beverly Sallee started out devoting 10 percent of her business profits to charities. Her goal is now to hit 50 percent.

At Diane's company, TaxLoopholes, employees donate time at projects including the homeless shelters in Phoenix, food banks, disaster relief projects, and orphanages in Juarez, Mexico.

Stephanie's Story

Stephanie, a Maui Millionaire from California, was one of the key members of a private equity fund called the Waters Fund. When she got involved with the Waters Fund she made sure that the fund donated a portion of its profit to charity before it paid out money to its investors. That original fund has grown into Waters Fund II. Last year, Stephanie raised $30 million for these two private equity funds and their 46 projects are generating a 45 percent annualized rate of return for their investors. As you can see, not only was Stephanie able to help her investors get a great return, but she raised a lot of money for charity.

But the power of her giving didn't end there. When giving is part of your business DNA, you never can anticipate the processional effects as that giving rolls out. Her example inspired Roger and several other Maui Millionaires to do the same thing on a large commercial real estate transaction they did in Denver, Colorado. Their project encompasses over 500 acres of industrial and agricultural land, including over 300,000 square feet of office and industrial facilities. Following Stephanie's example, Roger and his team have committed 10 percent of the profits from the founders' half of this large project to go to charity before any of the founders receive any profit from the deal.

You never know how your business's generosity will become a model or example for other corporations and businesses to give, too.

Turn Your Cause into a Business

One of the most successful alternative schools in California history was started when the founder lost his job as a social worker. He wanted to deliver results, and his supervisor wanted him to stick to the budget. The day he lost his job was one of those breakout moments. He knew he could apologize and beg for his job back so he could afford to feed his five children. Or he could go create the program he always wanted to—one that created real results for the students.

That was the beginning of Alicante School, a program that took the very hardest cases and provided education and counseling—mainstreaming 50 percent back into society. These were the kids that society had given up on. Most had already committed one or more felonies. Yet half of these kids went on to become contributing members of society.

One other part of his breakout thinking was that he didn't want to run the school as a nonprofit. Instead, he knew that the state of California had to provide education for children, no matter what the cost. He had a program that could more efficiently provide that education, and at the same time provide valuable life-coping skills. The business model worked. He became a rich man as he made a huge difference in the lives of others.

Do you have a cause that you are passionate about that could become a business?

Amy's Story

In 2004, Diane and her husband, Richard, traveled to India with Beverly Sallee to meet her business leaders there and visit some of her charitable projects. On one memorable day, Diane and Richard visited a huge jewelry store filled with diamonds, emeralds, sapphires, rubies . . . just about any fabulous gem you could imagine. They saw the most beautiful objects of Delhi. They then traveled with the group of Beverly's business contacts to a resettlement village located about an hour outside of Delhi.

They traveled on a dirt road, past a muddy river spotted with women in brightly colored saris washing clothes on its banks. The resettlement village was occupied by about 1,000 people, mainly women and children, who had been squatting in the bombed out buildings of Delhi. In a move of reconstruction, the buildings were being torn down and rebuilt in the city. The sick and weak occupants were taken out to this falling down village at an old mine site. The tiny rooms were built of rock with no windows and a hole where a door would go. There was no water, no sewer, and no electricity. The Americans were handed leis of fragrant flowers to block out the stench of the village.

(continued)

Amy's Story *(continued)*

They toured the abject poverty where the only employment available was prostitution. There was no transportation back to the city of Delhi where there were jobs. The people lived simply, perched in the hills, in a remote village where occasionally men came to visit the prostitutes.

The women begged for work, for anything they could to provide for their families. It felt overwhelming and impossible to the Americans.

That night Diane discovered a card from Amy for Beverly and slipped it under Beverly's door. At breakfast, Beverly was ecstatic. The card had included a check from Amy for $500 to be used wherever Beverly thought it would do the most good.

Beverly had the perfect use for the funds. It would pay for the initial inventory of material, thread, needles, and beads for the women to begin making beautiful embroidered and beaded products. Beverly had already contacted some of the wives of her Indian business partners to arrange a distribution channel for the products.

Today, Amy's Fund is known throughout the village, although Amy has never visited India or them.

It might seem that just a business began out of that small beginning, but what really happened was a chance for a new life for the previously hopeless inhabitants of a village by a mine.

Run a Business That Operates with Integrity and Gives Back in Nonmonetary Ways

David's Story

Over the years, one of the ways I've worked to give back to the world has been by mentoring and coaching my business team to succeed in their personal wealth building and become financially free. I've felt that it's a small but important way to pay back the help I've received from others. One of the special team members that eventually grew so successful he left my company was John. John was in his early twenties when we first started working together. Over seven years, he grew so successful in his investing in residential and commercial real estate that he transitioned out of working for my company. Together, John and I made a lot of money. Not only did we invest in millions of dollars of real estate together, but John was a guest speaker at several of my real estate workshops. One of my greatest joys is that for the past several years John has stepped completely out on his own and built up his thriving real estate investment companies.

Too many employers in my opinion are afraid of their team succeeding financially because they feel they'll lose good people. My advice is to mentor and coach your team to succeed financially anyway. Many of them won't have the courage or commitment of a John, but if you can just help a handful of them step up and succeed, you will enjoy a lifetime of satisfaction that you played a small but important role in their success.

Leverage Your Family

One of the surest ways to create sustainable giving is to teach your children to give as well. Look at the most successful people in life who started rich. It's easy to become overwhelmed by the financial success of your parents and their parents. That leads to a sense of "what's the use—I don't need to work" and takes away the purpose so important to children (and adults).

We all know the result of not having responsibilities and instead having a sense of entitlement—spoiled kids whose antics are splashed all over the tabloids. We also see the benefit of the instilled values from Family Legacy Giving. Get your children involved in more than just a one-time charity trip. Encourage them to meet and become emotionally impacted with your projects. Let them follow the causes that speak to them. It's more than just viewing third world countries so your children will "appreciate" what they have. It's helping them learn how to care and making connections that will keep the humanity in their own personal wealth-building and wealth-caretaking plans.

Steve's Story

Steve, a Maui Millionaire from Arizona, recently joined the Estrellas Para Ninos and Maui Mastermind for a weekend of giving and caring down in Juarez, Mexico. The most special part was that Steve brought his daughter Natalia and her friend with him. Can you imagine the impact on Natalia and her friend as they spent the weekend organizing and throwing a party for close to 100 kids from four orphanages?

Not only did Steve get to share this special time with his daughter, but he used the weekend to impart valuable wealth and life lessons, too. We urge you to look for ways to involve your children in your giving work, both as an opportunity to have fun together and to teach them about the joys of Maui Giving.

Leverage Yourself

The best way to sustain the giving for a worthwhile cause is to keep it fresh in your heart. Visit, in person, the direct recipients of the charity. Take along your family. In fact, how about changing your normal vacation from Las Vegas or Cancun and making it a visit to a third world country? You'll discover more about yourself then you ever knew.

Heather's Story

David's wife Heather is a psychologist. In the aftermath of the Gulf Coast floods, Heather volunteered to spend two weeks working with evacuees as a crisis counselor with the American Red Cross. She flew down to Texas and spent two weeks listening to people share stories of how their entire life was turned upside down in an instant. Those two weeks touched her in a way she never imagined possible. It changed her forever. She learned that she had an even greater capacity to care for others than she knew. But she also learned how important it was for her to care for herself along the way. In her past, her tendency was to give and give, and forget to nurture herself.

She came back from her two weeks, and nothing in her life seemed so hard or challenging anymore. She had so many blessings and such a fresh perspective that life felt crisper and more precious.

It's also important that you feel good about where you are putting your money and time. We recommend that you perform a Nonprofit Due Diligence before you invest time or money by asking questions like the following.

Questions to Ask a Nonprofit before Giving Money

Gather the following information with your White Hat on:

- The exact name of the organization (some sound-alike groups can be confusing).

- The organization's purpose (finding a cure for a disease, for instance, or caring for people who suffer from the disease).

(continued)

> ### Questions to Ask a Nonprofit before Giving Money
> *(continued)*
>
> - How the group attempts to achieve its goals (its own research, making grants, and so forth).
> - Where will the money go?
>
> With your Blue Hat on, look at the analysis of how they plan to achieve the goal.
>
> - Do they have the organizational experience and mindset to accomplish the goals?
>
> Finally, with your Red Hat on, how do you feel about the purpose of this charity? Does it speak to your soul?

If you can keep your heart in a cause, you'll support it.

Leverage Your Future

Who do you want to be? The vision you have of yourself can change the moment you open up to thinking beyond your personal desires. It becomes more than just making your dreams come true, but extends beyond to making the dreams of others come true.

Beverly Sallee is known for her philanthropy. Here is what she says sustained giving means to her.

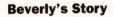

Beverly's Story

Every time I write a check, or give a speech or give part of my business away to support a cause, I say, "I know what sorrow is. Let me stand with you in your sorrow."

I was raised by parents who had gone through the Depression. They saved everything because they felt they might need it in the future. It took me a while to realize that hoarding means that you have no trust in the divine providence that you will be taken care of. When you give to widows and orphans, you are giving to God.

I do a lot of work in other countries and so besides the limiting beliefs about wealth that Americans have, I hear a lot of other limiting beliefs. For example, in India, it's felt that you need to follow everything your parents say and do because that's how you honor them. That type of thinking will lock you into repeating your parent's lives. Instead we look at ways to evaluate the beliefs that we've learned from our parents. Of course, still honor your parents, but do it without taking and believing everything they did.

In fact, my parents told me not to go to India, that it was too dangerous. If your parents are giving you ideas that don't stretch you, that encourage hoarding and not sharing, maybe it's time to examine those beliefs.

I've had a number of epiphanies in my life. One of those occurred when I went through a divorce and felt I needed to consciously change who I was going to be.

My goal now is to give away 50 percent of what I make and live on 50 percent. The money flows in faster than I can spend it. I find I can't even spend the money. Getting one more trinket just doesn't have the same appeal anymore.

Beverly's strategies for creating a Big Dream for a charitable purpose:

- *Keep your dream in mind.* "If it's not the right time, the right players will show up eventually and then it will be the right time. I dreamed of turning my 17,000-square-foot house in Washington into a safe retreat for abused women. A divorce took that dream away. But now, years later, a friend has a hotel where women know to come in and ask for a 'book of matches.' That's the code to receive a purse, phone card, and personal items to get them going. Another friend is running the Tacoma (WA) Rescue Women."

- *Do due diligence before you give your money.* "I want to see something already in place that is getting good results. I would rather come alongside someone working, than try to do it myself. I tried to do a lot of things with people who were just beginning their projects and found that there were many people who didn't know how to manage people, money, or projects."

- *Know who you are dealing with.* "They might be good people, but they may not be able to handle money or the responsibility of the project."

- *Plan to give and save right from the beginning.* "A good program in the beginning is to plan to give 10 percent and save 10 percent. Don't live on 100 percent of what you make. Build giving from the very beginning. As you get more, give more."

- *Build a relationship with the people with whom you partner.* "It doesn't matter if it's in business or in charitable business. Build a relationship where you genuinely care about the individuals and families you work with. If you find you don't want a relationship with them, then maybe they aren't a good fit in your other businesses."

- *Always practice sustained giving.* "How can you make sure that your giving lives beyond your lifetime? Think 50 years out and teach your children and grandchildren how to continue the work you set in motion. Find financial institutions that will manage your giving in accordance with your wishes. Finally, design ways to create residual income streams for the charities and causes you believe in that will continue to flow year after year."

Giving back can change your personal and business life. You come alive when you do something without the hope, desire, or expectation of getting anything in return. And yet, somehow, you always *will* receive more than you give.

PART SIX

THE FINAL INCH

CHAPTER 21

The Fourth Dimension of Wealth

David had a friend who several years ago broke the world record for the 400-meter individual swim medley. David's friend touched the wall just a few *hundredths* of a second before the second place swimmer that day.

On July 27, 1993, high jumper Javier Sotomayor broke the world record by *less than a single inch*.

In sports, in business, in life, we consistently find that the difference between the best and the rest is measured in that final inch.

The final inch is what turns the ordinary into the extraordinary. The final inch is what transforms a millionaire into a Maui Millionaire. It's a life filled with nurturing relationships, good health, spiritual fulfillment, great wealth, and above all, the time and freedom to enjoy these blessings.

We've talked about how to create a field of multiple Big Dreams to inspire a full life. But there is still one more piece—the final inch—to add the finishing touch to your wealth. We call it the fourth dimension of wealth.

The Fourth Dimension

The fourth dimension adds the quality of duration to your wealth-building plans. You might remember from science class that there are three dimensions present in our physical universe—length, width, and height. The fourth dimension is time. Of course, we all are time travelers—it's just that we go one day every 24 hours in a forward motion.*

But now let's consider something else: how to add the fourth dimension to your wealth so that it becomes permanent in your life.

There are three elements to time: past, present, and future. The present is right now. Everything we have discussed so far is designed to bring you more in line with being present with what is truly going on. You've identified your own W.O.S., learned about Level Three wealth, identified your Big Dreams, and formed a mastermind group. Now let's look at how to extend your wealth into your past and future.

One more comment about time. We often think that wealth building is slow, that change requires massive amounts of time. If that is your paradigm, then you are absolutely correct. But consider the fact that Texaco bought Getty Oil in one weekend, start to finish. The Pentagon, the world's largest building, was built in 13 months. Anything is possible. Time is not an issue. Put the focus and the resources behind it, and time is not an issue.

Many Maui Millionaires made their first million in less than 36 months. Others did it in less than 36 weeks! And most made their second and third millions even faster. Time and time again, we've watched Maui Millionaires perform miracles that average people said just couldn't be done. When you have your choice between safe failure and leaping for success, we hope you take the leap of faith. No matter what the outcome, you'll find your life enriched.

Gratitude—Wealth in the Past

When you show gratitude for where you are now, you are giving conscious attention to what you have in your life. It expands your perceived

---

*For those physicists out there we recognize that we're simplifying the model of the known universe to exclude quantum mechanics and relativistic breakthroughs, but, hey, the analogy will make you wealthy in powerful ways, so cut us a little slack, okay?

wealth. It's as if you had awakened to see all that has been given to you in your life by God, however you define that to be, and the people around you.

Imagine that tomorrow you wake up to discover that over the past 10 years, an eccentric billionaire has been depositing money into a safe vault, in your name. Now, suddenly, you learn that there is a whole lump of cash just waiting for you. Not only that, but it's been waiting there for you anytime you wanted it for the last 10 years. You are now a billionaire.

Are you rich now? No matter how you define middle class versus rich, we probably all agree that a billionaire is rich. So, no problem there. But, how about last year? Were you rich then? Yes, even though you didn't know it. You were rich the year before that and the year before that and the year before that. You've been rich for years and didn't even know it. That's what showing gratitude for the things in our lives is like. We suddenly wake up and discover we had more wealth than we ever knew.

We started this book with an exercise that put a value on your life. Now, let's put a value on the things you've been blessed with by first acknowledging what is true in your life.

Gratitude Exercise

Write down five things you are grateful for in the first column. Next to each item, in the second column, write why each item is so important to you. And in the final column, write what action you want to take to demonstrate your gratitude during the next 24 hours.

What I'm Grateful For	Why I'm Grateful	Next Step
_____	_____	_____
_____	_____	_____
_____	_____	_____
_____	_____	_____
_____	_____	_____

Do the Gratitude Exercise each day for one month. You might even want to include your family and review it together each evening. It becomes a very positive, uplifting way to end the day as a family.

Gratitude adds the past into the fourth dimension of wealth. Now, let's add the future.

Giving—Wealth in the Future

Giving is such a significant part of being a Maui Millionaire that we included a whole section on it in this book. But, there is one more reason why giving is such an important aspect. It adds your solid certain belief that you will be wealthy in the future. When you give, you avoid hoarding and that means that you have faith that you will continue to be able to have wealth in the future.

As soon as you begin to hoard for the future, you are saying that you don't believe you can have more in the future. Now, again, we're not saying don't save. We're saying don't let saving stop you from giving.

Here is an exercise that will help you stretch your giving muscles.

Giving Exercise

Assume that you have one of three choices for giving. You can give $10 per day, $100 per day, or $1000 per day. This is a commitment you will make right now, today, for an entire year. Which one makes you gulp? Which one stretches you beyond where you are? It doesn't matter how big the number is. Your goal is to find the one that makes you gulp. Oh, if $1000 per day isn't enough, it's okay to make it $10,000 per day, or $100,000 per day.

Now, write that number down:

I pledge to give $_____ per day to charity for the next year.

X_____   _____
                             Signature   Date

The next step is to consider where that money will go. What causes will you support? Take another piece of paper, and brainstorm what difference that would make for that cause. If you are giving $10 per day (or $300 per month) you can sponsor 10 children with World Vision, for example. What difference would it make for 10 children to receive needed food and medicine? What kind of an impact would you have in the world?

This needs to be deeply personal. Push yourself to put your heart into the exercise.

Now find a partner, and, with your Blue Hat on, explain the plan to make this happen.

Finish with the Red Hat to explain why this is so important.*

Ultimately, gratitude and giving stretch your wealth into the past and future. They enhance your wealth by adding the fourth dimension of *duration* to your wealth.

In the final chapter of the book, you'll learn how to put the ideas you've learned so far into practice so that you quickly put yourself on the path to become a Maui Millionaire.

---

*If you are really committed to becoming a Maui Millionaire then go to **www.MauiMillionaireBook.com** and click on the "Maui Giving" tab. You'll find examples of various charities you can work with to take this exercise and make it real.

CHAPTER 22

A Simple Six-Step Plan to Become a Maui Millionaire

Congratulations on making it through the book to this final chapter. It's a big accomplishment because it not only means that you invested the time to read the hundreds of pages of wealth creation ideas, but more importantly it means that you have embraced the ideas of creating wealth Maui-style.

Now it's time for powerful and productive action to take that next step on your personal road to wealth.

Over the last few hundred pages, you've learned dozens of strategies and techniques to build wealth and become a Maui Millionaire.

You've learned how your W.O.S. determines your ability to grow, maintain, enjoy, and share great wealth. And you've learned the five steps to upgrade your W.O.S.

You've learned the 25 keys to dreaming big. And you've learned the five essential ingredients to make those dreams come true.

You've learned about the awesome power of a mastermind group. And you've learned how to effectively harness that power to succeed at levels that previously seemed impossible.

You've learned a new model of wealth. And you've learned how to use this knowledge to chart your progress towards Level Three wealth and living the Maui lifestyle.

Finally, you've learned that real wealth isn't what you make, it's what you share. And you've learned how to leverage your giving to leave an enduring legacy that lives on beyond your lifetime.

Now, in this final chapter of *The Maui Millionaire*, it's time to get into action. We've designed a simple six-step action plan for you to follow to accelerate your wealth building and become a Maui Millionaire.

This action plan has three layers to it.

Layer One is the book itself. It is the sum total of all the concepts, exercises, stories, strategies, and technologies we've shared with you in these pages. But this is just the starting point for your wealth creation. There are still two more layers to the action plan we've designed specially for you.

Layer Two is a powerful free bonus we've spent thousands of dollars designing, testing, and building. It's called the Maui Millionaire Wealth Mentorship Program™ and this breakthrough 90-day online wealth mentorship program will literally take you by the hand and walk you through—step-by-step, action-by-action—exactly how to transform the ideas in this book into tangible results in your life as fast, easy, and enjoyably as possible. It includes dozens of online tools, workshops, and wealth-building shortcuts to make building wealth Maui-style a done deal. And it is our *free gift* to you because we believe that you were born to make a difference.

Layer Three, the final layer, is your real-world application of the ideas and concepts you've learned from us. Ultimately, it will be this last layer—you—that is the magic ingredient that breathes life and wealth into all that you've been learning.

Are you ready to take this final step? We thought so! Let's do it together!

Step One: Upgrade Your Wealth Operating System

As you learned about in Part One of this book, it is literally impossible for you to build, maintain, enjoy, and share great wealth unless you have a W.O.S. that supports this abundance. Therefore, the first leverage point to building your wealth is to fine-tune your W.O.S. so that it is a highly functioning, powerfully programmed, lightning-fast, irresistible money magnet.

To do this you have three action steps.

Action Step One: *Immediately register for the Maui Millionaire Wealth Mentorship Program.* Once you've registered, take the online Wealth

Factor Test™ so that in five minutes or less you'll know exactly what your current W.O.S. is set for.

Action Step Two: *Participate in the online W.O.S. workshop.* This simple, free workshop will take you by the hand and walk you through the process to upgrade your W.O.S. as quickly as possible.

Action Step Three: *Finish the exercises you read in Part One of the book.*

Step Two: Uncover Your Big Dreams and Make Them Real

What are your real Big Dreams? Why are they so important to you? By clarifying what matters most to you, and getting outside support to make those dreams real, achieving and enjoying success and freedom is easier and more doable than you could ever imagine.

To do this you have two action steps:

Action Step One: *Play the Maui Millionaire Big Dream Game.* Simply gather a group of three to seven people you care about, enjoy, and respect, and have a blast playing this powerful game. To download your free copy of the game, just go to **www.MauiMillionaireBook.com** and click on the "Big Dream" tab. (Note: You can leverage this action step by combining it with Step Three: Forming a trial mastermind group. To do this, simply play the game with your mastermind group!)

Action Step Two: *Re-read Part Two of the book and finish the exercises you read there on dreaming big.*

Step Three: Form a Trial Mastermind Group for a 90-Day Test Run

Remember, you are literally one mastermind group away from every dream you've ever wanted. This is your chance to take a test spin with a trial mastermind group and learn from the real world exactly how to harness the amazing power of a focused mastermind team.

To do this you have three action steps.

Action Step One: *Brainstorm a list of 10 potential mastermind teammates you would like to approach to form a mastermind team with.*

Narrow your list down to five to seven people. Give each of these people a copy of this book to see if they want to play the game of life at a higher level in the spirit of Maui. If they haven't read the book in two weeks, then move on and find someone who is more committed to building the life of their dreams.

Action Step Two: *With your entire mastermind team, participate in the online Masterminding Basics workshop.* Just have each mastermind team member take the workshop and then set up a time to meet in person or via phone to discuss the workshop and lay out the purpose and ground rules for your own mastermind group.

Action Step Three: *Meet with your mastermind group at least once every two weeks for 90 days.* At the end of that time, openly discuss as a group what you liked best about the experience and what you'd like to do differently next time. Collectively decide if your group has the right chemistry to continue, or if you should all go your separate ways each having learned and benefited from this trial run.

Step Four: Master the Concept of Level Three Wealth

Level Three wealth is about creating the passive, residual income so that you win the money game and become financially free. In order to do this, you must first master this new way of looking at wealth, find out exactly where you stand financially, and regularly chart your progress as you build your financial fortune.

To do this you have three action steps.

Action Step One: *Participate in the online Level Three Wealth workshop.* This workshop will reinforce and clarify the key components to Level Three wealth and how you can shift your wealth-building efforts into alignment with this powerful and effective model.

Action Step Two: *Take the Keeping Score workshop.* This online course will walk you step-by-step through how to know exactly where you *really* stand financially, and how to fine tune your wealth-building efforts along the way.

Action Step Three: *Teach at least two other people about the concept of Level Three wealth and the Maui Millionaire Financial Freedom Formula.* It's a little-known secret that as we teach we learn and integrate at a deeper level. This one step could literally make the difference for your financial future.

Step Five: Commit to Maui Giving

If you get nothing else out of this book other than the lesson that you become wealthy by what you give, you will lead a blessed life. Determine where your passion to help and contribute is, and commit to making giving a natural part of your daily life.

To do this you have three action steps.

Action Step One: *Participate in the online Maui Giving workshop.* This fast-paced, inspirational workshop will help you clarify exactly how individuals like you can change the world. It will also walk you through a simple process that will make Action Steps two and three much easier.

Action Step Two: *Determine what charities or causes you are most passionate about.* The place to begin your giving is with what moves you emotionally. Brainstorm the groups and causes you care most about. Don't worry, you can always change your focus later, as your heart and conscience directs. Pick one group or cause to start with.

Action Step Three: *Commit to a definite percentage of your time, talent, and money to give to the world.* How many hours per month on average will you commit to help others? How much of your talent and skills will you commit to leveraging to help the causes you believe deeply in? Where will you plant your money to grow seeds of good fortune for the world? Now get out there and live your word.

Step Six: Connect with the Maui Wealth-Building Community

You've learned that character is contagious and that your ability to build, maintain, enjoy, and share great wealth is greatly enhanced when you are in regular contact with like-minded, positive people. That's why we founded the Maui community. Join us, and together we can accomplish more, enjoy more, and share more.

To do this you have three action steps.

Action Step One: *Immediately register for the Maui Millionaire Wealth Mentorship Program.* Once you've registered, you'll get information on how to become part of the online portion of the Maui wealth-building community. You'll meet other people at various stages in building their wealth, and you'll be able to help each other do it the Maui way.

Action Step Two: *Join us twice a year for a Maui Millionaire Wealth Weekend.* These semiannual weekend workshops are a time to meet in person and renew friendships, network, and learn the latest strategies and wealth-building tools from David and Diane and the Maui Stars who volunteer to be there. All proceeds—*gross* not net—go to charity. All the hard costs of the event itself are paid for by Maui Millionaire, LLC, so that every dollar raised by the modest ticket price goes to charity. These powerful weekends have become a way to not only raise hundreds of thousands of dollars for worthy causes, but to also accelerate you on your way to financial freedom. To find out more about these events, just go to **www.MauiMillionaireBook.com** and click on the "Live Events" tab.

Action Step Three: *Share your new commitment and action plan for building wealth Maui style with at least three people over the course of the next 90 days.* This can mean sharing your Big Dreams with someone you care about. Or it could be e-mailing a friend with a link to the **www.MauiMillionaireBook.com** site for them to check it out for themselves. Or it could even mean mentoring a friend you care about to share the concepts you've been learning about. Remember, Maui Millionaires all care about building their wealth in a way that brings other people along with them. Besides, by taking this action step you will be creating a peer group of people to support you in your wealth building!

Closing Thoughts

As we told you in the beginning of this book, the road to wealth won't be easy or smooth. There will be bumps, sharp turns, flat tires, and even a few confusing moments where you might lose your way. But hang in there anyway. In the end, the journey is infinitely worthwhile, and the detours and challenges along the way can sometimes be the best part.

You've got one life, and it was given to you as a gift. What you make of it—the passion, the creativity, the joy, the generousity, the laughter—is how you show your appreciation for this priceless gift.

We are humbled that you have allowed us into your heart and life for the time we've shared in this book, and we wish you real wealth *along* your journey, not just at the end of it.

If you ever doubt your capacity to keep on the road, then borrow our faith. If you ever find a step too scary, then let us walk beside you in spirit, and together we'll take action in the presence of your fears.

You are a lamp of greatness, and the world needs your light. Embrace your power, live your dreams, share your good fortune. You will never have the chance to relive this moment, so make it count. You are a gift in our lives, and we treasure you for it.

David and Diane

The Maui Millionaire Wealth Mentorship Program— Your FREE $2,495 Gift from the Authors

Dear Reader,

As our way of congratulating you for finishing this book, we've created a unique online wealth mentorship program just for you that will walk you through—step-by-step—exactly how to put the wealth-building ideas from this book into action.

We want to be clear here. We are giving you the tools to become financially free, but you are the one who is going to have to do the work.

Are you serious in your desire to be wealthy? Do you truly want to put the ideas and strategies in this book into action so that you can enjoy the time, wealth, and freedom you've always dreamed of having? Then we urge you to take the next step and claim your free $2,495 bonus right now.

To register, all you'll need to do is go online to **www.MauiMillionaire Book.com** and use the access code:

Freedom33

When you register online you'll get immediate access to this comprehensive 90-day wealth mentorship system. It's designed to help readers like you master the ideas in this book, and to quickly and easily put your wealth building on overdrive!

A Surprising Secret
That Few Readers Know

You may not know this, but the original draft of this book included dozens of extra stories and several extra chapters, all of which had to be cut for the sake of space. To be frank, it was heartbreaking to cut out so many wealth strategies and stories, but we had to do it anyway.

But since we aren't the type of people to let a small challenge like the space limitation in a book stop us from sharing all that we wanted, we decided to put all that extra content up on the Web for you to get as a free bonus.

Actually, we didn't stop there. Rather than just give you the extra text, we took it 10 steps further and turned that extra content into a complete online wealth mentorship program that you get for free. Here are the details of what you'll get *free* for a limited time as part of this special gift to readers like yourself:

What You Get as Part of This Valuable *Free* Bonus:

- **Ten online wealth workshops** that will make building your wealth *easier* and *faster*!

- **Free download** of the Maui Millionaire Big Dream Game. Gather a group of friends or your mastermind team to play this game and you will automatically be upgrading your Wealth Operating System!

- **Private access** to video footage from Maui and the charity efforts our graduates engage in!

- **Personalized assessment** of your current Wealth Operating System through the use of a proprietary tool called the Wealth Factor Test.

- And much, much more!

You'll Also Get *Instant* Access to 10 Free Online Investor Workshops:

Workshop One:	The 7 Foundational Wealth Skills of the World's Wealthiest People!
Workshop Two:	How to Build Level Three Wealth and Become Financially Free!
Workshop Three:	Masterminding Basics—12 Techniques to Tap into the Real Power of Your Mastermind Group!
Workshop Four:	5 Simple Strategies for Valuing Any Business!
Workshop Five:	The 9 Most Powerful Tax Loopholes!

Workshop Six: Keeping Score—How to Use the Maui Wealth Scorecard to Accelerate Your Progress to Financial Freedom!

Workshop Seven: The Vision and Values Workshop—Five Steps to Create a Compelling Future!

Workshop Eight: Wealth Lessons from the World's Most Generous Philanthropists!

Workshop Nine: Simple Steps to Upgrade Your Wealth Operating System!

Workshop Ten: Level Three Leverage—15 Techniques to Build More Wealth with Less Time and Effort!

Best of all, you'll be able to attend all these workshops from the comfort and convenience of your own home!

Here's How the Maui Millionaire Wealth Mentorship Program Works!

Step 1: Go online to **www.MauiMillionaireBook.com** to register using the access code:

Freedom33

Step 2: Take the Wealth Factor Test to determine exactly what your current Wealth Operating System is set for and to learn the three greatest leverage points to upgrade it.

Step 3: Take the Maui Millionaire Intro Class that will share with you exactly how to use the Maui Millionaire Wealth Mentorship Program™ to grow your wealth and freedom. It will give you the specific steps to take to accelerate your wealth-building efforts so that you immediately begin to grow your net worth and cash flow.

Step 4: Follow the 90-day action plan and take all of the FREE online wealth workshops. Also enjoy the other powerful wealth tools and resources that are available to you on this private web site.

Step 5: Tap into the Maui Community, both online and at our semiannual live conferences. Get involved networking and masterminding with other like-minded individuals so that together you can accomplish more than you dreamed possible.

10 Reasons to Go Online and Register Now!

1. This special bonus offer is available for a limited time only and may be withdrawn at any time. You'll kick yourself if you miss out on this opportunity!

2. The ideas and strategies you'll learn about business and investing are the most certain paths to financial freedom!

3. The sooner you log on and get access to all the powerful information and wealth tools, the sooner you'll start building your wealth!

4. The Maui Millionaire Wealth Mentorship Program will help you get out of the rat race and become financially free!

5. We just may come to our senses and start making people pay for this valuable bonus! (In fact, we reserve the right at any time to start charging for what this valuable bonus is *really* worth.)

6. The sooner you start building your wealth, the sooner you can start sharing your good fortune with other people!

7. It will help you take your wealth building to the next level!

8. It will inspire you to take instant action!

9. It will help hold you accountable so that you make money, not excuses!

10. You'll build so much momentum by reading the book and logging on now you'll literally be propelled to greater levels of success!

Register Within 30 Days and Get the Following Special Bonus!

When you register within the next 30 days of buying this book you'll get one more special bonus—exclusive access to more than *six hours* of private recordings of the interviews we conducted with the Maui Millionaires featured in this book! This extra bonus is available for a limited time only.

Imagine listening to these private, one-to-one interviews, and hear exactly how the Maui Millionaires really built their wealth, what obstacles they had to overcome, and how they would do it differently if they had it to do all over again.

Register now and you'll get to learn the best way possible to build your wealth, by modeling the known success of these powerful wealth role models.

You'll learn:

- How one Maui Millionaire increased his effective net worth by 1,000 percent in less than 36 months!

- The one belief that held another Maui Millionaire back from financial freedom, and how when he changed this one belief he went on to buy over $20 million worth of real estate in less than two years!

- How an ex-corporate consultant went from three weeks out of every month on the road to becoming a financially-free Maui Millionaire!

- And much more!

How to Register for the Maui Millionaire Wealth Mentorship Program—FREE!

Simply go online to **www.MauiMillionaireBook.com** right now and complete the enrollment form. When prompted for the access code simply enter:

Freedom33

It's literally that easy!

Again, we thank you for reading this book. We wish you a lifetime of success and happiness. Enjoy your "graduation gift" of the Maui Millionaire Wealth Mentorship Program!

Our very best to you,

David and Diane

P.S. To get your Maui Wealth Mentorship Program ($2,495 value), simply go to **www.MauiMillionaireBook.com** and register now!

P.S.S. We urge you to register now because this offer is for a very limited time only and we'd hate for you to miss out!

David Finkel

In a cluttered marketplace of "how-to-get-rich" books and infomercials, ex-Olympic-level athlete turned business and real estate multimillionaire David Finkel is one of the nation's most respected wealth masters and the co-creator of the exclusive Maui Mastermind™ wealth retreat.

David first retired after selling off his successful multimillion-dollar company at age 35, but he soon grew bored with the quiet life. Taking advantage of his fresh start, David carefully chose what he was most passionate about, and then launched and built two multimillion-dollar businesses that focused on that passion—distilling the real rules of wealth and sharing those skills and strategies with ordinary people to help them create extraordinary wealth.

David's mission is to share the real story on how to build wealth that debunks the prevailing money myths that keep so many good people living below their real potential.

David teaches people around the world how to Get Rich, Get Real™ through building businesses, investing in real estate, and making the *real* commitment required to be rich in all areas of your life.

David is a prolific author of over 30 business and investing books and courses, including *The Wall Street Journal* and *BusinessWeek* best seller, *Making Big Money Investing in Foreclosures Without Cash or Credit.* His how-to financial articles have appeared in over 4,000 periodicals across the United States.

David believes that true wealth doesn't require hard work, but rather the right kind of work, focused on things that really matter—to you and the marketplace.

He is a wealth realist who helps people realize what is *really* required to get rich and reach their personal and financial goals.

He and his wife Heather first met in San Diego, but now live part of the year in Jackson Hole, Wyoming, and part of the year in Charlottesville, Virginia.

His web site (**www.GetRichGetReal.com**) is the home of one of the most popular wealth blogs on the Internet.

Diane Kennedy

Diane Kennedy, the nation's preeminent tax strategist, is owner of Diane Kennedy & Associates, a leading tax strategy and accounting firm, and founder of TaxLoopholes.com, a tax education company. Diane is the author of *The Wall Street Journal* and *BusinessWeek* best sellers *Loopholes of the Rich* and *Real Estate Loopholes*, and co-author of *The Insider's Guide to Real Estate Investing Loopholes*, *The Insider's Guide to Making Money in Real Estate*, and *Tax Loopholes for eBay Sellers*.

Diane's extensive teachings have empowered people throughout the country to minimize their tax liabilities through the use of legal tax loopholes.

Diane has written for numerous financial publications, and has been featured in *Kiplinger's Personal Finance*, *The Wall Street Journal*, and *USA Today*, and on CNN and CNBC.

A highly sought-after international speaker and educator, she has dedicated her career to empowering and educating others about financial investments and the tax advantages that are available. Through Diane's knowledge and execution of tax loopholes in her business and real estate investments, she and her husband Richard are able to contribute to special life-changing projects and charities in the United States and around the world.

For the latest expert advice on tax loopholes and critical tax law updates, as well wealth building resources, visit her web site: **www.taxloopholes.com**.